Voices along the Road

ISBN-10: 1979555680
ISBN-13: 978-1979555685

Voices along the Road

A collection of poetry and flash fiction in aid of the
Alf Dubs Children's Fund.

For all those seeking sanctuary

CONTENTS

FLASH FICTION

About the Charity

Lord Alfred Dubs arrived in Britain in 1939 as a six-year-old refugee, one of thousands of Jewish children who arrived in Britain on the Kindertransport. As an adult, he has campaigned tirelessly for refugees.

The Alf Dubs Children's Fund aims to help child refugees find safe and legal routes to sanctuary and to ensure that the children's basic needs are met while their cases progress, as well as supporting them during the first stages of their lives in Britain.

We decided to put together an anthology to raise money for refugees in 2017, after the Dubs Amendment was dropped in parliament. The amendment sought to bind the government to relocate and support 3000 unaccompanied child refugees.

As of publication date, only two hundred children have been brought to Britain under the Amendment and many more, who are eligible to settle in the UK, remain stranded in refugee camps or on city streets.

Originally there was only meant to be one book, but we had such a great response from writers wanting to get involved that it quickly expanded into two: *Voices along the Road* collects flash fiction and poetry, and *Another Place* is a collection of science fiction short stories.

All of the stories and poems you'll read in the anthologies have been donated, and all of the authors, poets and editors involved have waived a fee for their work.

The book is not officially endorsed or produced by Citizens UK and Safe Passage, or The Alf Dubs Children's Fund, but all profits will be donated to the fund.

You can find out more about the Alf Dubs Fund at:
http://safepassage.org.uk/what-we-do/alf-dubs-fund/

POETRY

.

IMMIGRANT

Olga Alexandru

I don't know what it's like to have olive skin
in a country so pale
it never occurred to me it was different
so I tell myself, inhale

I know what it's like to wish
these brown eyes blue
because it's what I envied
wished for, too

I don't know what it's like to be Jane or Sarah
but I know what it's like to have extra letters in my name
that are undecipherable
without strain

I know what it's like to have English as my fourth language
but have it be the first now
to feel the lack of my mother tongue
and so often wonder, how?

When eyes are on me
I know what it's like to act tough
to keep the expression off my face
when you say this country's not big enough

I don't know how to be Romanian and Canadian at the same time
to not fit firmly in either box
to reconcile the in betweenness
so I wish someone would just open the doors and locks

AUSTRALIAN CHILD MIGRANT

Rosalie Alston

Buff- coloured folders
thumb-stained cream pages
David
Maureen
John.

Automatic typing
dates and decisions
Christopher
Margaret
Peter.

Brothers and sisters
in separate houses
Anthony
Teresa
Michael.

'I think I met her once,'
he said.

'I think they showed me her
through the glass door
when we walked past the nursery;

when we walked across
the Downs to school
before I went to Australia.

'They showed me a map,'
he said.

'They showed me a flag,'
he said.

WHO I AM

C.B. Baker

Who I am:

I am the wind

Dancing across lands, across hands that carry me so

I am the sky

Wakened by a dawning fire, prancing carefully in its shadow

I am the water

Trailing across grounds, hoping that I will be found

I am you

Fleeing from the hating, the pulsating fury that sounds

Wishing to come home

A TASTE FOR FREEDOM

C.B. Baker

There's a drum in my chest

Thudding, beating, throbbing, fleeting

There's a voice in my head

Speaking, yelling, hurting, meaning

There's a life in my body

Running, hoping, wishing, wanting

There's a taste in my mouth

Sweetened, bitter, broken, beaten

There's a soul in me

Yearning only to be free

CLOSE

C.B. Baker

I'm home

Can't know it yet

Can't see it yet

But I know

The food

Can't smell it yet

Can't taste it yet

But it's there

The people

Can't meet them yet

Can't love them yet

But they're here

The life

Can't live it yet

Can't feel it yet

But I'm close

FOREIGN BABIES

Angie Belcher

What if all immigrant babies' Britishness had to be proven?

Dear baby Orwell, Freedom is slavery but nappy is damp
Do you think the future is dystopian? Cos you look a little blank
Will life mirror art with your past thoughts now being how we think
But for now let's get your teddy and another milky drink

No Brunel, put the Lego down, and stop that teether gnawing
You look a little short to be of use, and your English is appalling
We're gonna need some trains and bridges, Do you think you fit the bill?
Surely no European son can navigate our English hill

Oh Freud, we think your obsession with your mother's tit is terse
We can't have such phallic nakedness travelling round our universe
But we don't want an Austrian teaching psychology forces
And no, that's not a slip of the tongue meaning I want to get friendly with
horses

Stop right there Handel, you're not the messiah
Answer the question, take out that pacifier
Cos Hamburg might be the best place for your little overture
I'm afraid we find you playing chopsticks a little immature

Oi! TS Eliot less of this goo-goo gaa- gaa
We're a little cautious of writers from afar
Let us go then and I, there's Nobel Prize competition to beat
I'm not sure a state-side child can write about a British street

Marx, stop playing with your bits, and that comfort blanket has gotta go
We're looking for someone dead clever to write a radical manifesto
But we don't think no frenchie can understand our politic
Oh, go get a bib, Baby Karl has just been sick

Wake up Tolkien, no time for fantasisers
We may need some classic wordly writers
But that South African accent gets on our nerves
You won't be able to teach us about Merrie middle earth

And where is Henry James, Is he scribbling again?
He won't be able to write about the themes of love and pain
What is it again? Oh another portrait of a lady?
I think we'd better get an English child and dismiss this Yankee baby

Kipling! that bell's for me and not for you
How will you discipline yourself to write a story or 2?
I'm not sure an Indian can write with an English heart
You stay there and practise vowel sounds and eaugh, did you just fart?

THROWN INTO THE STORM

Linda M. Crate

---

little girl
weight of the world
on her shoulders,
little boy
eyes swimming with tears
he should not know;
they are victims of a war made by
people who should know better but let their
greed be bigger than hearts
who closed their palms and made a fist rather than
offered their hand to help—
you should never look down on anyone
except to help them up,
but they try to crush people they don't know into dust;
slander them and criticize things they cannot
hope to fathom
whispering secrets that aren't even true to incite panic
in people perfectly safe—
but these children are shivering with doubt
their futures unknown
relying only on the sea to guide them somewhere safe
a haven who will shield them from a storm they should have
never been pulled into.

YOU CAN'T DO THAT

Linda M. Crate

the world is on her shoulders,
she doesn't know
how she'll breathe again
if the next dawn they face will be
their last;
she's a mother who feels
like she's failed
yet it's the world who failed her
threw her into the eye of a hurricane she should
have never had to face—
war makes losers of us all
no matter who wins
we all lose something: a piece of our humanity, a piece
of our family, a piece of heart;
something's always taken that we cannot return
maybe she'll find her peace of mind
but not any time soon—
today she just hopes she and her children can find
a safe place
shielded from the wings of a war
that sought to take her life
because a handful of greedy men decided to put a price
on a human life
but you can't do that.

TOGETHER WE RISE

Linda M. Crate

it makes my heart heavy,
makes my heart sick
that people can do evil things to
one another without care
even take pleasure in it;
one cannot put a price tag on the life of
another human although funeral homes try
we're all worth more than they say
because we are all made of stardust
we have the power to aid others and use our tongue to heal
instead of ripping down and destroying,
and so i will not stand for this world of nightmares;
people need safety, hope, and dreams
so that is what i will give them
because my heart is a lighthouse hoping to bring every ship
who needs aid its help
because we all need someone to lean on
none of us has ever built ourselves up entirely alone
together we rise but divided we fall.

A RAFT IS NOT A COUNTRY

Tim Burroughs

---

a raft is not a country
dry land is just a dream
refuge would be welcome
refusal is obscene

a shoe is not a child
and a life jacket
did not keep him safe
he drowned like all the others
trying to escape

they are just normal people
same as you and me
scared out of their minds
by bombardment and ideological extremes

their fate is all more real
if you're of mixed ethnic blood
your people once fled fascism
and the baying lynch mob

'cos when you're clinging to a raft
with a thousand miles to cross
with forty shivering refugees
your life has the same value
as those safe on the quay

CHAIR

Richard Devereux

An Army-issue chair, held stacked in store,
kept ready for Emergencies like this –

it smiled at the refugee and welcomed him,
invited him to stop, sit down and share.

He ached the ache of walking, sleeping rough,
to such a man, a simple chair's a throne.
It took his weight and he became as light
as an infant held in an angel's arms.

He undid the laces and eased off the boots.
He wondered what they were, those stumps he saw

as he unwrapped the stinking, soggy mulch
of sock – those raw and bloodied feet, once his.

He heard the right and left compare their tales
of all the way they'd come, remembering

the stony roads, the stream they'd crossed in flood,
those nights they just kept walking on till dawn.

Reacquainted with his feet, and with himself,
the man got up and nodded his regards
towards the chair. He joined the queue for food;
a friendly face exchanged a smile with him;

a tent, a bed, a pack of simple things.
        And then he started wondering – what next?

JACK AND AMER

Hannah M Rudd

Jack is 11 and ¾
After school he falls from trees and khaki streaks his starched uniform
When the days are long dad forgets bedtime and he cycles the streets
under a chalky moon

Amer is almost 12
His friends play football near a water pump, taking turns,
they use their water butts as goal posts
When gunfire spits and cannonball cracks Amer pretends
Jack Sparrow is hunting treasure

Plump ladies with rough hands give Jack lunch on a tray
A plastic trench plugged with cutlery sears through the centre
On one side there's a crater for peas, on the other,
ditches for mash and meat
'Why can't I have a plate?' Jack asks
Jenny, (his best friend) doesn't mind,
she likes her peas separated from the mash

Amer use to stare at the men with big hands, (hairy like his fathers),
tensed around triggers
The rest of their bodies were bound in khaki
'It's hot. Why do they wear so many clothes?' Amer said,
his cotton shorts and vest flapped in the breeze
His father's fingers, (tentacle wrapped around Amer's arm)
leave marks of mottled mauve

Ear pressed against a doorframe Jack hears about a boy
Wearing shorts and a vest he'd gone to the beach
on a plastic dinghy
But he wasn't on holiday
and he shouldn't have been there
Jack doesn't think he made sandcastles.

HE COMES TO ME FOR COMFORT

Gerard Twomey

He comes to me for comfort
With some small hurt or fear.
My embrace seems inadequate
For what my heart feels,
But for him it is somehow enough
And sorrow soon forgotten
He turns to something new.
He knows no reason;
Bedtime comes and goes.
He bites and twists like a cat in a bag
I feel the judgement of soft denizens,
His fuzzy familiars like gargoyles
Now in shadow, phantasms made of night.
Sleep is smothering,
He fights until he succumbs
To my cobbled rituals
And half remembered words
Culled from rhymes and songs.
Still in my arms, he rubs his hand, warbling
'Why aye aye aye,' over his fetish, my nose.
A dream might wake him or a cough
The monitor amplifies every cry and murmur
And the LED rainbows into the red
As we bend jaded ears and tense:
It could go either way.
In the morning a sad litany:
"Mama here?"
No, Mama's at work.
"Me no go playgroup."
"No change me nap, Da da."
The stairs suddenly become an obstacle
As he notices a cobweb outside the window
"Carry me dada, caa me" emphatically,
With arms outstretched and toes curling
Teetering too high up, on the top step.
He'll fling heedless into my arms,
Knowing I'll catch him.

SUPERHERO

Helen Sheppard

Department states a minor arrives
At her door a sparrow boy appears
He drops empty into a flat pack city
Sleeps tonight where no bullets fly
Dreams
It's dark
Water ice
Black fins of shark
Their languages don't match
At breakfast she cooks him eggs
He pinches clouds of sour dough
As petals they float in his bowl of warm milk

PORCELAIN

Helen Sheppard

Waif of a girl with a porcelain face, waits
for a boy, almost a man with an easy smile
He makes her laugh.
Says she's worth knowing.
At fourteen and a half, she's ready for love.

He tells her to fly.
In a car they ride away from city lit streets.
She tries a toke, from a spliff.
He says breathe.
Hold in your throat, feel mellow, act bold.

He tells her to smile.
Gives her a phone, all contacts his own.
She answers day, night whenever he calls.
He makes her play.
In a line they leave her battered and torn.

He tells her to die.
Best left for dead. Her soul in a mess.
Months never found.
One day, warm breath on her lips.
Her rape angel grows.

Feather down wings pierce, then unfurl.
She takes flight.
A sickle of moon catches her throat.
This grace of a girl screams,
shatters her porcelain face.

TRANSITION TOWNS

Merlin Goldman

They were sent to Transition Towns
to fil anodyne buildings with life
Hara, Flowing Chang, Revelation,
Darling Khan, and Chaos
Abandoned by others
these buildings would not reject them
Unwanted, uninvited
this was their mercy

BEFORE YOU DIE, YOU GROW SO OLD

Gavin Ritchie

I was a boy in June; by July I was
an old man being taken to Chelmno.
Moon faces beside me passed under shadows,
aged fast, like dropped apples, pecked and opened to the flesh

by time, fast falling through the rail car floorboards.
Passing Kutno station – slowing over knuckles in the tracks –
we tip-toed to see the tall, two-storey building. It had
rounded glinting windows and bright yellow walls.
The dried-up children with us could not reach
the barred white slots we gaped through,
could find no care for the passing places
that passed our time; they were already
old, knew more than I did, how I trundled
toward July from my farmstead home, Lidice.

BROTHER

Clive Oseman

He lives his life above the law
with repression and brutality
practised ruthlessly as if they were the norm
as people turn their back on such insanity.
His wife, a mere metaphor for slavery,
controlled and chained.
His children chided, beaten, molested, maimed
if protests dare be heard.

When his eldest son escaped,
stood crying at a neighbour's gate
hungry and in pain, he got sent back..
A garden is a private place
a never to be invaded space-
The neighbour knew the score.
Give the child an inch,
he'd take much more.

So fences were electrified, security intensified
The children may be terrified, abused,
but never being asked for help
is better than refusal, right?
These kids could share ridiculous beliefs,
indoctrinate the others on the street.....
their suffering's a worthwhile sacrifice
when our own little nirvana is complete.

That's nonsense, you say.

Now stretch the scene around the globe
see masses of innocents in the same boat,
call them refugees or immigrants,
not seeing any difference.
Would you now ignore their plight?
Refugees are nothing
but brothers, sisters, husbands, wives
with desperately shattered lives.

Depending on their neighbours, to survive.

SCENT OF *QAHWA*

Tara Lynn Masih

Because desperate men fight always to control something—
this time it is *ma'a*, the water as it disappears—
this girl will fight through leech-filled swamps,
forge the vast White Nile,
watch sisters go down in crocodile jaws.

She will survive on rainwater,
green flesh of shea nut,
salty porridge of tree leaves,
while skin swells with ticks and
shreds in Kono thickets.

This girl will reach the refugee camp on petrified feet,
find neither food, nor water.

She will stay, fight a kind of death
behind the camp's truck barriers,
wrestled down, voice smothered in tall grasses
by three militiamen.

She will not sleep,
must listen, listen for sounds of
helicopters, MiG's, and approaching *janjaweed*.

Under a Sahara-stained tent,
this lost girl will fight to remember
the scent of *qahwa*,
the vision of a mother's desert-dry hands,
dusted in grindings of clove and fried coffee beans,
offering her family their daily drink
in tiny clay cups.

RETICIENT MUSES

Paul David Holland

How might they sing, these birds caged in their gilded prisons
If released to the sweet mindlessness of this new freedom,
Tasting the openness of unsummoned adventure?
A loyal obedience glints in every glance, a flickering suppression
Of honesty fading to the truth within, a weary acceptance,
Shackled to the land they did not choose.

Instead, exile and solitude lurk about the dark horizon,
Solemn conclave of portent-heavy clouds,
Grim warnings from Ovid and Brecht of time soon stretched
Taut with the needs of existing, the daily routine crowding in,
The tasks not attempted, the unchallenged hope forever stifling
This life to be lived, this nightmare to be undreamt.

But here and there the delicate tendrils of the dispossessed and
Unpossessing push out, tentative yet strong;
Like the buds of late winter striving towards the light
These pack a tight weft of punch, the surprise of a foetal glance,
Defending a memory of what's left behind, seeking salvation
In their knowing escape from a gathering chaos, but loathing still
The sudden, cold release to an unbidden world,
Words dense with the rawness of sight,
Coiled in upon themselves,
Sprung with unfettered, pure aggression:
They'll have your eye out if you get too close.

EXPULSION FROM EDEN

Paul David Holland

What is it you dislike about the fragrant pathways and idle lawns
Here on this small patch of planet tamed and styled for pleasure?
Princess of far-off realms replete with over-hallowed courts and halls,
Names which ring with ancient myth, and dance across our pages
With all that brilliant, exotic distance that dusts our past,

Wander this garden and be soothed; for it too is haunted by voices
Echoing across blood-soaked millennia, cities and sandscapes scarred
With the lives of all those whose tales you and I shall never know.
Here amid the safe bowers of summer's bright pageant,
Anemones, jasmine, roses in raucous riot,
There waft the ghosts of furthest myths and legends,
Untroubled by their own world now sinking in the mire of war and waste,
Bleached with despair and resigned to some new cycle of loss.

I'll offer these to you, poppies blazing with the searing scarlet
Of half-pious remembrance and collective guilt;
And these perfumed lilies that wreathe the catafalque
In place of mourners (so few survive – those that do are far away)
For once we also mourned our own fall, and fled, and came to know
That so much of what we loved could never more be whole,
So much shattered, a lost innocence mourned in nostalgia
Thick with selfishness.
                        Oh, the anger which swirls about your loss!
I feel it too. But like an unruffled god glancing at his ticking watch,
Helplessly my only gift is patience – and this sweet space to rest.

In hours yet to dawn beyond your time perhaps and mine
There is peace; exhaustion it may be, a final, all-too-human sighing
At the waste of so many years; or it could be the light of reason
Breaking through like sunshine over all the countless paths to take!
But it will come, it always will. And these tears will help no-one,
Nor your indignant fury.
                        It takes a tide of loves and lives
To shift the hearts of others, so trust instead the present, sit here awhile;

By no new truth can you hope to nudge nations from their course,
And Eden is long lost too, that much we know.
Stay and be at peace here. This is no Eden, but its gentle paths
Streaming with life and comfort offer the only gift worth taking.

The Paradise you seek is not behind you but ahead,
Yet to rise from the stark, stony scrubland still unformed.
Watch the rooks in the high trees all about; they'll give a sign;
Like the gardens we tend, we are mostly nature untamed,
And gardens need work. Eden was never lost – we were.

BOY ON THE BEACH

Luke Palmer

There were fruit trees outside our house.
One day they were gone so we left and now
I am here. I do not know what brave is. The others

tell me I am brave and let me keep my shoes.
They seem kind. They showed me
where the fruit trees are but they are not the same —

their fruit falls apart in my mouth like sand
and tastes of salt. I have lost my father.
I am always wet. They say that is how things are

no matter how hot the sun. I ask
if we have escaped. They won't answer.
Sometimes I talk to the water. It tells me

I am a thin skin with the sea on both sides.
It says I am a wave that has broken.

THE YOUNGEST DUST IN A GLASS COFFIN
Oradour Sur Glane

Luke Palmer

Before they came I was toothless and dove-light.
My body, limp with too much skin and un-fused bone,
could not yet tighten as I milked my mother's breasts.
My red-mouthed hunger. *Michèle Aliotti - petite chérie.*
Perfect as God and exhausting as the other.

When they came and called us out I had to be woken,
unstirred by trucks and boots. My mother's arms
and milk scent roused in me a cry that fell
to her shoulder, my fury rag-loose and impotent.
She wrapped herself around me and cradled me to church

where, as screams and bullets rang against the walls, she smiled
at me, her hair around my face, around my useless, flailing arms;
her hair around my dove light wings that burned.

ASYLUM

Mary Prior

I love this England.
I love the rain,
the petrol rainbows in the puddles
as I buy my Pepsi
from the garage shop.

No guns, no bombs.
No one is trying to kill me.

The English are strange.
They ask me, 'Do you miss the sunshine?'
But I don't.

I don't miss the sunshine
or the fear or the despair.

I am just glad to be here,
to feel the rain on my face
under the safe, grey sky.
I have a roof over my head
and food in my belly.

I sleep safe at night.

I love this England.
I love the rain,
the petrol rainbows in the puddles
as I buy my Pepsi
from the garage shop.

THE LEAP OF FAITH

Mary Prior

Have courage, he says, have hope - we must leap.
I clutch my children, as we flee the guns.
He holds my hand tightly, don't weep, don't weep.

They stole our money, but we try to sleep.
The sea moves round us, as I sooth our sons.
Have courage, he says, have hope - we must leap.

The boat is sinking and our lives are cheap.
We, the worthless, the despicable ones.
He holds my hand tightly, don't weep, don't weep.

Lost my boy dragged into the sea, so deep
My hope, my joy, just a child the world shunned.
Have courage, he says, have hope - we must leap.

We're pulled out of the sea, a naval sweep
Warm food and sympathy, the kindness stuns.
He holds my hand tightly, don't weep, don't weep.

Herded like animals, we stumble and creep.
My baby is wailing, high fences, more guns.
Have courage, he says, have hope. We must leap.
He holds my hand tightly and I weep and I weep.

FOLLOWING

Mary Prior

Patchworked soil, packed hard, burning hot
Horizon disappearing into whitened sky.

The boy's head is bowed.
Swollen feet placed carefully
to avoid the cracks, the ridges
that scrape his calloused soles.

His mind is swollen
with buzzing images,
like locusts, like hornets
swarming incoherently,
round and round.

Doggedly, he follows the ant trail
of his tribe
across the wasteland
past desiccated corpses
of abandoned livestock.

He must keep up.

He concentrates
one foot, then the other
step by step.

REBUILD

Saili Katebe

We piece together fragments,
Making whole again the peace.
Striving to firm our courage,
Through courage, revive relief.

Trinkets of golden splendor,
Have survived the final pass.
The final flash of coursing water
Did not dilute the past.

The present presents us brilliance
Through resilience we remain.
The chains to a blooming jewel
That sustains our people name.

How strange today may seem
Through the echoes of what was loud.
Now resigned to live in whispers,
That whimper in foreign shrouds.

Cast steadily into the morrow,
We borrow the gifted hymns.
Hopeful strings of songs we sing,
To secure our second wind.

BARRIERS

M M Lewis

you deserve better
I would give you
ice creams with sprinkles
sun shining through branches
swings and slides
dizzying roundabouts
splashing in paddling pools
spinning falling over
playing by
lakes with plump ducks

you deserve better
but we must be apart
there is a safer place
an ocean separates us
forms and signatures
statutes of law
lack of funds
quotas and frowns
concrete and glass
rivers roads and tracks
voters and taxpayers
who newspapers say
don't want us
at least
they don't bomb us

THE SHORE

M M Lewis

The past, like the sea:
Memories wash out
Like withdrawing fingers
Raking wet sand
Until the sea is a blur in the distance
Like the old country.

The past, like the sea:
floods back in
no matter how tight
you hold on
The waves will grasp you
Pull you down
Sweep you away

Until you're washed up
a thing left on the beach:
bone dry but not yet home
driftwood
a bottle without a message
A gasping fish drowning in air.

BEAUTY AND THE BEAST

Michelle Marriott

Multiple Choice: The Eurotunnel

1.
A long transparent glass tunnel bathed in dazzling light,
like an aquarium, where small silver fish swirl and shimmer.
You sit snugly in the bucket seat of your little purple Peugeot,
which smells of yesterday's discarded burger wrappers,
watching elegant stingray glide through swaying seaweed.

2.
A long, reinforced concrete tunnel immersed in darkness,
perforated only by flickering strobe lights that fizzle and buzz.
Your purple Peugeot rides in the carcass of a high-speed train,
where air-con recycles spores from mouldy burger wrappers,
and you hear the industrial screeching of metal on metal.

3.
A long, cold breeze block tunnel shrouded in grey gloom,
where a shuddering conveyor belt moves you slowly onward,
pulling your little purple Peugeot through the polluted smog
which smells of diesel fumes, and greasy burger wrappers
discarded by weary motorists with churning stomachs.

PUMPKIN

Aziz Dixon

She runs, she dances,
shrieks with delight,
bonfire will smudge her,
Cinders til midnight.
Spiders, ghouls, witches
and sprites, and a pumpkin
too good to eat,
candle-face fear,
but Mummy is near,
she'll be alright.

Night shivers him still
in the wolf-picket jungle.
Toe stirs numb embers.
All hell flickers.
Dead brother, dead mother,
dead sister, dead lover,
hand claws dust-white in the rubble,
hunger-pain place.
He could thieve for a pumpkin,
roast in the flames.

THE INDIAN STONE

Tony D'Arpino

The house near the forest
Dreaming
Around the corner of green

The boy said here
This is an Indian Stone
Thanks I said

I wasn't much older
His beautiful barefoot parents
Smiled when he gave it

A long narrow stone
Marked with a line
Of bright blue chalk

I have it still
In my desk like a saint
My first forest gift

LAST JOURNEY OF THE ANONYMOUS

Lisa Lopresti

A beautiful sea beckons us across,
All hearts open and squeezed as those on board,
So full of fear and hope the boat awash,
Wishing, wishing to move safely forward.
Fleeing war: now one more trip of peril.
This is the last risk we tell ourselves,
Made vulnerable to those who are feral.
Courage and strength that each one has to delve,
Vehemently praying all will be right.
Wishing, wishing no bereavements this night.
Immigrants – They have had enough!
Aylan and Galip gave a face to us.
Our greatest hope, Europe is waking up?
Now poor lads, we are not anonymous.

SYRIA SEQUENCE

P.J. Reed

---

face hidden home lost
she walked into the desert
clutching her white cat

a drought of bullets
man pushes heavy handcart
as his children sleep

white helmet searcher
pulls baby from under home
and both are crying

THE DEVIL SLAKES HIS THIRST

Lindsay Oliver

The devil dons his mask
and casts our children from the land
with promises purloined from
the nightmares of the dead

The devil sheds his skin
walks the dark sequestered streets
as we worship and adore
his glory all unbound

The devil stakes his claim
to pitch his shadow on the sea
while we collect his rent
from the safety of the shore

The devil takes his due
with an unforgiving hand
more practised than restrained
and lays his burden down

NOT MY CHILD

Lindsay Oliver

Not my child
Laying limp in the sand
Face down in the sea

Not my child
Huddled unbreathing
In a cargo container

Not my child
Stranded alone
Dead on a beach

Not my child
The curl of his fingers
The curve of his cheek

Not my child
Hair soft as thistledown
On the nape of his neck

CHRISTMAS, SYRIA, 2015

Lindsay Oliver

Our anger at those who sit
and vote, decide your fate
will not diminish your parents' grief
nor quell your grandparents' fears
we have no balm to offer

Unto us a gift was given
We returned it
spurned it, denied it
before the cock ever crowed

Christmas, Syria, 2015
On this day, a child was born

FLASH FICTION

REPRESENTATION OF SOUND

Benjamin F. Jones

The tree has arthritis, its roots scrabble into cliffs painted with rust. In search of solitude a man uses it as a place to rest, he's old and his wishes expired years ago. He leans against the trunk and tries to work out where his body stops and the pain begins. Nightfall draws warmth from rocks and a family out walking stir the shadows at the back of his heart. The girl he loved was lost on the journey but he still holds the poem he wrote for her, its words are angular, tough as olive bark. They drill into memories coloured with sunburn and spray. Out at sea kids play on the wreck of a bean-can trawler. The flat rays of the sun stick to the hull and waves become a representation of sound. With no rush to listen, voices tumble on the cusp of day and night. It's twenty years since he arrived, but for two heartbeats he thinks the laugh he can hear is the one he lost.

WAVES

Tanya Almeida

Mama, Papa and me, swishing in the sea. Sabah stays on dry land, building castles in the sand. I try to get him to swim, hold his hand and walk to the sea. But he screams and runs away when waves wash over his feet.

We used to go there each day, my favourite place by far. We stopped when bombs rained down, no longer safe to play. So I watched the waves from my window, dreamt of floating free, wished for cool blue sea, away from summer heat.

Soldiers came that winter, took my Papa away. Mama never stopped crying, people kept on dying.

Clinics ran out of medicine, bombs wrecked our shops and school. Mama said we must move to a land with safety and food.

We sailed in boats with our neighbours, floated gently out to sea. Then it got dark and scary, boats crashed around in the night. Waves got bigger and bigger, we clung to Mama in fear. Sabah screamed as we bounced around, as waves washed over our heads.

Boat went over, we went under, it was dark and cold in the sea. I swam as hard as I could, hoping Sabah also would. When I surfaced I grabbed onto Mama, but Sabah was not to be seen.

Strangers came to our rescue, speaking words I couldn't understand. They wrapped us in blankets, took us ashore. We tried to tell them about Sabah, but our words made no sense to them, a babble of foreign sounds.

Now we are safe in England, just Mama and me in our flat. I'm the only Syrian in school, the only girl named Yana. They talk about Daddies and brothers, I never say a thing about Papa and little Sabah, lost to horrible war.

Today is our school trip to Weston, eating ice-cream on the pier, riding donkeys on the beach, building castles out of sand. My friends try to get me to swim, hold hands and walk to the sea. Nobody knows why I scream when waves wash over my feet.

SAFE PASSAGE

Maggie Elliott

For the past few months, my environment has been calm and serene. Although totally dependent on someone else for protection and development, I am flourishing, because I have warmth, comfort and all the nourishment I need provided on demand.

Nurtured by a very special person, I am kept in a perpetual state of peacefulness. My guardian's voice is soothing and comforting. Although I cannot see them and do not understand what they say, the sound is always welcome, soothing. The bond between us is powerful.

Living in complete darkness, I use my hands to feel my way around and can tell that my home is compact, bijou, but appears to be decreasing in size recently. Movement has become difficult.

Presently I sense big changes. Movement is restricted and there is a change in the tone of my guardian's voice. No longer soothing or comforting, it is strange, loud, fearful. Compelled to travel in a direction I don't want to go, there are other voices, shouting. I am being forced down a very tight passageway. Pressed and released repeatedly. Eventually ejected into a world of brightness and harsh noises, I am introduced to a new environment with a slap which makes me wail.

Having survived safe passage into the world, I am almost blinded by light the first time I open my eyes. The sights and sounds that envelop me daily are sometimes overwhelming, but I have no sense of fear. The peacefulness and tranquility replaced by wonder and awe.

Although totally dependent on others for protection and development, I am flourishing, because I have warmth, comfort and all the nourishment I need provided on demand, here in a refugee centre.

ESCAPE FROM THE JUNGLE

Clare Evans

The noise was the worst thing: a constant din of alien tongues, arguing, fighting, trying to gain precedence. Jungle by name, jungle by nature. Escape to England was his only desire.

He kept his eyes low. He saw their feet, in mud-encrusted trainers, before he heard them.

"Boy? Boy?"

He swallowed, and tried to walk past. A large hand with dirty nails and an iron grip grabbed his elbow. He tried to shake free but they surrounded him.

"Come with us. We're going to get on a lorry tonight."

Hamid looked up, keeping his hands in his pockets. They were barely older than him but their glittering eyes under sweatshirt hoods hid what they'd endured. Empathy was absent.

"You are Afghan too. We will look after you."

Hamid stared at the boy-man with the bruised face, carrying a nail-studded plank of wood. He shook his head. They wanted him because he was small and had a better chance of launching himself at a lorry and opening the back. He'd tried this route before and seen the weapons used to frighten the drivers. That was how his brother died. Now he was in this hell-hole alone.

"No." His voice emerged as a croak. "You go. I don't want to."

They crowded him, breathing poisonous fumes over his small face.

Hamid ran. He was never safe. They would return, or others like them.

He hid behind an empty container until his breathing returned to normal. He heard the call to prayer but didn't risk following it. Not yet. Normal rules were suspended here.

The Jungle was going to be dismantled and what little stability they had would be gone. It was a structure, not a home, but better than total anarchy. There were possibilities: food, clothes and charity workers.

But danger was in every shadow.

As a child, he had a chance. He'd seen more than a man should experience in a lifetime, fighting his way from a broken Afghanistan, through the people smuggling routes and across Europe. Here, he'd found a different kind of hell.

He needed to get to England, to join their legendary uncle Ghazi. It was their plan, until Taj fell off the back of a lorry and Hamid was left in this zoo alone.

*

The buses were here. He lined up with the others, almost all boys, many with their hoods up to disguise their age. No one could dispute that he was a child.

An official with a clipboard ticked the boys off one by one and they climbed the steps into the coach. Even those who looked older were accepted and Hamid relaxed. He could almost feel the touch of the plush seats under his fingers. He managed a smile when it came to his turn.

The man in charge searched for Hamid's name on his list, frowned, and turned to a second page. He consulted with another man standing beside him. Hamid felt a hand on his shoulder and he was pulled out of the line.

"You are Hamid, travelling to join your uncle Ghazi?"

"Yes."

There was some kindness in the man's face, but not enough. "I'm sorry, Hamid, but something has come to our attention this morning."

"Has something happened to uncle Ghazi?"

"Hamid. How long is it since you saw your uncle?"

"It is several years. He has said I can come. I know he has." Hamid felt the terror rising. Nothing could go wrong now, when he was so close.

"Your uncle has been arrested, on terrorism offences."

"No." Tears streamed down Hamid's face. "Uncle Ghazi is a good man."

"I'm sure he is, son, and it may be a misunderstanding. Perhaps he has been keeping bad company. He will receive a fair trial and is innocent until proved guilty."

"So, I can still go?"

The man put his arm around the boy's shoulder. "I'm afraid it's not that simple. He will be remanded in prison. There is no home for you to go to."

"What can I do?"

"You will have to stay here, while it is being sorted out."

Hamid felt a flame of anger in his chest. "How can I do that? The camp is being demolished."

Despite his own anguish, he could see the desire to help in the man's face. Now was the time to fight, to plead, to get his foot in the door. "Don't leave me here. I am alone. I am frightened. Please help me."

"There is an expression in Britain, better the devil you know."

Hamid looked back at the Jungle. "The people who say that have never known a devil."

THE LAST DAY OF OUR TIME

Karolina Kew

On the last day of our time the sun rose at precisely 5.43 in the morning. I know this because for once I was awake early enough to see it.

I'd had an anxiety dream about J. We were supposed to meet up for dinner, but instead I ended up lost in a field and couldn't find my phone or him, or something. That's nightmares for you.

I didn't really fancy going back to sleep after that so I got up and made a pot of coffee. My nervousness had nothing to do with J and everything to do with the job interview I had that day. Leaning against my kitchen counter, surrounded by the smell of the finest dark roast money could buy - in the local supermarket, I was rehearsing answers to the questions I'd ask if I were on the other side. That's when I noticed the sun rise. It showed up in a halo of colours and sudden beauty that surprised me out of my worries for a while. I vowed to make the effort to wake up in time for this more often. Not an unusual reaction to accidentally witnessing a sunrise, I think.

Done with the coffee, I turned on the news and left the bathroom door ajar so I could brush my teeth to the sound of important people in sombre voices gambling the world away. There was footage of a conference with thinly veiled threats and back at the studio a reporter earnestly questioning an expert while I paired a navy-blue jacket with my favourite shirt and tied my hair up. As I flipped one last time through my notes, a grey suited leader of the nation J belonged to looked straight into the camera and placed it all on red.

I left home with plenty of time to spare, aware of the traffic problem that'd been intensifying in the city for some weeks now. As expected, several streets around the centre were closed off and as I drove by I could see some people already gathering for a demonstration.

The office block looked a little corporate but at the reception desk I was greeted warmly by staff of assorted genders, ages and ethnic backgrounds. There were tv screens in the lobby showing that same man in grey, his face angry in close ups, and a growing crowd of protesters chanting angrily as if trying to make themselves heard over the mute function. I was getting nervous again now that my time to shine was nigh.

I knew I was more then competent for the position, just never been best at what's called 'selling myself'. The phone chimed in my pocket, first with Good luck my love, then Dinner tonight, my treat. Whatever the result and the thought of J thinking of me was miraculously calming. I texted back See you on the other side and headed for the interview.

I guess one day, very soon now, when we're just smudges of crowd in the background of a historical photograph, the future 'us' will shake their heads and say of J and me: Didn't they know what would happen? How could they not have known?

In the evening, I chose to leave my car at home and take a taxi to the restaurant so I could have a drink to celebrate. When I arrived, J was standing outside. He opened the door and helped me out of the car and we kissed. He said he'd only just arrived himself, but I think he must have been waiting there a while just so he could make that gesture.

Over dinner, I told him about my interview and that I thought it went well. I remember saying: after all I only embarrassed myself a little and at the very beginning. I remember both of us laughing at that.

Now I think I'd have liked the job. I'd have liked the view from that corporate office block, had it not vanished in a pile of dust. The man who'd interviewed me said they would let me know the following day.

On the last night of our time I went to bed feeling pleasantly drunk and though I can't remember the dreams it seems unlikely I would have dreamt about the future. The loneliness of the one-way journey surrounded by strangers or the rubble left behind, lifeless bodies of friends rotting in unmarked graves. Instead, I like to think I would have dreamt about J again. Even if it were a nightmare. Nightmares were never quite so bad back when I could still hope to see him again.

The next day it was too cloudy to see the sunrise and anyway that was the day war broke out, and just like that our time was done.

TOKYO VIOLET

Merlin Goldman

When the cold sores appeared on Talib's neck, Violet tried to hide them. They were a side effect of cloning and if she took him to a hospital, she might never see him again.

In 2046, the UN delivered a final ultimatum to North Africa: stop the exodus of migrants or they'd switch off the geotractors. The League of North African Nations introduced a one child programme but most ignored it. They began sterilising the male population. Those that refused, lost the right to work.

Mother was one of the first clones. She had chronic asthma and a failing cardiovascular system. But such was the compulsion to have a child, thousands of mothers and fathers copied themselves. The cloning protocol was shared like recipes for one pot chicken mafé, each one improving on the last. Governments confiscated machines but they couldn't stop it.

The first verified death occurred a week after Mother's sixth birthday. The suicides were initially considered to be acute postnatal depression. Except it happened to both parents.

Scientists called it Mirror Rejection, an evolutionary safeguard. When the first parents handed in their clones, they were arrested. So they abandoned them on the streets. Violet found Talib watching street football.

Mother took them all in. She sent the youngest to work in vertical farms, growing modified tea plants. They scuttled up and down plastic ladders, picking the buds, laden with stimulants.

When old enough, Mother smuggled them by boat to Japan and as long as the children arrived undetected, they were ignored.

They became Budonoki, meaning vine. They provided an extra layer of protection on top of the Assisted Living Machines that cared for the elderly – the Furui ki, old tree. Only the richest could afford both.

Mother steered them through the shipping channels to avoid UN patrols. Every few hours she handed each of them a soap-shaped packet. Talib pulled off the wrapper and frowned at the crickets embedded in the clear, sugar coating.

"It's always the same," he whispered to Violet.

"Just eat it."

"What do they eat in Japan?" said one of the other children.

"Raw fish," said another, gnawing at a corner.

"Seaweed."

"Noodles."

"Whatever it is, it'll be better than this," said Violet. They all nodded.

"Will they love us?" said Talib.

"They'll have to," said Violet. "We'll be keeping them alive."

Mother craned her thick neck over their heads. "Hold on tight."

The children gripped the edges of the benches and turned to face the autonomous vessel. It slid past tall and silent as a giraffe. The wake hit the boat. Some screamed. The boat dropped then rocked. Water flopped inside.

"I'm scared." said Talib, pushing his hip against hers.

"I won't let you go."

The waves diminished and the children relaxed. Between ships, they played mancala using the food wrapping as marbles. Their shoes became cups.

Violet dabbed sunscreen onto the pale scars on Talib's neck while he scanned the water. "What are you looking for?"

"Whales."

"There's none left. Now turn your head."

Mother examined the sun's glare reflected from the polished metal tower. "We'll be there tonight."

Mother let the boat drift in on the current. They huddled together under the blue metal sheet as perimeter drones buzzed overhead, until finally the boat shuddered as it scraped against the ground. The cover was whipped off. Pale men pulled the children out, pushing them into a van.

After an hour's journey, most fell asleep. They arrived at a farmhouse as dawn hinted its arrival. They were carried upstairs and slept on evenly spaced mats on the floor. Mother paused in the doorway, blocking the light. When she shut the door, Violet pulled Talib's mat next to hers.

Violet woke first and tiptoed through the cold house. The yeasty odour of last night's miso soup lingered . Mother was gone. Violet ran outside but was dragged back, marshmallow pink petals sticking to her feet.

Every morning, the children were taught Japanese. In the afternoons, they wore VR headsets to run simulations on different Assisted Living Machines.

One morning, Violet found one of the mats empty. The following week, another. The pale men told her nothing.

Violet woke on the backseat of a windowless car. Alone. The thick, cream panels swallowed her screams as hungrily as her kicks and punches.

Her Furui ki promised to help her find Talib and bring him to live with them.

During the day, the Assisted Living Machine monitored her health, recording data from sensors embedded in her clothing. At night, Violet attached the Assisted Living Machine's tubing to her, cleansing her blood as she slept.

Mieko had been a famous actress, married to a J-Pop singer. She was a hundred and three. They acted out scenes from her most famous films. Mieko told her that that secret of acting was to never break from your role.

On Sundays, they visited Rikugien Garden where Mieko had been married. Violet programmed the wheelchair to follow the wedding party's route, stopping at the ornamental pond so Mieko could gaze at the floating lotus flowers.

When she fell asleep Violet would cross the small bridge to visit the Mochi ice cream stand. The owner always treated her to a small cup of red bean flavour. She'd asked him to look out for her brother.

Today, as she approached, he pointed to the pond's edge. A white-haired woman was feeding the ducks, watched by a black boy sitting on a bench. Violet ran. It wasn't Talib.

"Are you a Budonoki?" she said in English. He nodded. "Do you know where my brother Talib is?" He shook his head. "I need to find him. He's coming to live with us."

"Furui ki's never have two."

It wasn't difficult to make it look like a malfunction. She told them an osmotic sensor had failed during the night. The skin on Mieko's arms looked like the corrugated iron huts that lined the roads into Nairobi.

Violet continued to cry long after they'd shut the van doors. She hoped the next Furui ki would be more helpful.

SEARCHING FOR KANSAS

David Turnbull

The Scarecrow was roused at dawn by the pecking of the crows. He shook away the glistening crust of frost that caked his raggedy clothing. The crows scattered, cawing boisterously. He scanned the nearby farmhouse. When he felt certain that no one had yet risen, he set off with a lolloping gait through the muddy furrows, shedding bits of dislodged straw as he went.

He was alone. A stranger in a strange land. A week ago, he and the Tin Woodman had watched helplessly from the hillside as the Lion was chased through a valley by vicious dogs and shot dead by the hunters who seemed incapable of defining him as anything other than a grotesque monstrosity.

Two miserable days later, they had been caught out in a thunder storm with no shelter. The Tin Woodman's joints had rusted frozen. The oil they'd brought was long gone. All the Scarecrow could do was abandon his friend by the side of the road, covered by leaves and branches.

Leaving Oz had been the Tin Woodman's idea.

"Home," he'd said as the Lion scavenged for scraps of food in the battle-scarred ruins of the Emerald City. "We should go there. Dorothy once said there's no place like it."

It hadn't taken much to convince them. Oz had been brought to its knees by years of civil war, faction fighting faction, coven against coven, huge swathes of territory under the authoritarian control of the dreaded Wiccan Fundamentalists. The ethnic cleansing of the Munchkins a bloody and shameful stain on the pages of history.

They'd crossed over from Oz under the cover of a raging gale, Kansas bound, wind howling, the Scarecrow and the Tin Woodman sheltering beneath a gaudily painted banner that had once belonged to the Wizard, the Lion trembling with fright, tail curled up between his legs.

"There will be a road," said the Tin Woodman. "Just as the Yellow Brick Road used to lead to the Emerald City, there will surely be a road that leads to Kansas."

But every road they followed led them nowhere.

They naively believed that people here would be as kindly as Dorothy had been and they only had to ask for directions. But wherever they wandered, they encountered bigotry and hostility. It seemed that no one in Dorothy's world had anything but contempt for anyone whose appearance was in any way in the slightest different.

In one particularly nasty town, they had been stoned by the locals. Huge rocks rained down on them, accompanied by jeers and hateful taunts, the Tin Woodman's breastplate all battered and dented, a huge hole in the Scarecrow's belly, where a jagged rock had passed straight through the tangle of straw. It had taken a desperate and ferocious roar from the Lion to make their assailants scatter and flee.

Later, skulking in the sidings of goods yard, they had actually debated returning to Oz.

"In my heart of hearts," said the Tin Woodman. "I know that I could never return."

"Deep down," sighed the Lion, "I am as cowardly as I ever was. I would easily surrender to one or other of the covens and allow myself to be indoctrinated."

The Scarecrow had cogitated a moment before speaking his mind.

"I suppose I am clever enough to pretend to be radicalized. But I'm also smart enough to know that it would be a terrible idea to try such a thing."

Eventually they'd agreed that home remained the best option and began exchanging little snippets of information they had each gleaned about this mythical place.

"It's where the heart lies," said the Tin Woodman.

"It's where the deer and the antelope play," said the Lion, licking his lips.

"It's where everything seems to be right."

They remembered a song they'd heard about someone who longed to be homeward bound and laughed at the serendipity of the fact that they were ostensibly sitting in a railway station.

"It's a good omen," said the Tin Woodman.

The Scarecrow thought it was more like the scattered piece of a jigsaw puzzle.

Now he was alone and, for all he knew, still a million miles from Kansas.

He looked down at his mud-caked boots. The mire of the fields was slowing him down. At the bottom of the hill, there was a narrow, twisting road. It was still early. The morning mist hadn't lifted. He surely wouldn't run into anyone.

But fate, in her contradictory manner, dictated that someone ran into him.

He had only been walking along the road for ten minutes when one of the four-wheeled contraptions that plagued Dorothy's world came roaring round a bend and sent him tumbling violently into the air. He landed badly, stick limbs all twisted, stuffing well and truly knocked out of him.

A long time passed before he heard the sound of chattering voices and tramping feet. A whole procession emerged from the mist; men, women and children, all as ragged and shabby as he. They didn't baulk at the site of him. No one swore or tried to hit him. Not one of them walked by as if he was invisible. A man knelt down at his side. His face was gaunt and unshaven. His eyes seemed haunted. "Can I help you, brother?" he asked.

"If you could gather up my straw and stuff it back inside my clothes I'll be fine," he replied.

The children gathered the straw.

"Where are you headed?" asked the man.

"I'm not entirely sure," replied the Scarecrow. "Somewhere in Kansas, I believe."

The women set about stuffing him with the straw.

"Kansas is long way away," said the man. "Do you know exactly where?"

"Home?" he replied.

The man helped him to his feet

"Brother," he said, "in one way or another each one of us is searching for home."

The procession set off once more, chattering and tramping.

The man turned and beckoned to him.

After a moment, the Scarecrow followed.

BEACHCOMBING WITH KAFKA

Tony D'Arpino

To Tarn

The car was missing again. I found it in the park by the sea. It had a flat tire, which I pumped up with the bicycle pump. I noticed someone had left a crab in the front seat. It wasn't a crab exactly, but a kind of crustacean, and one I knew very well.

He spoke. "O, wow, you understand me."

"Yeah, we're sentient creatures."

"What I don't understand is how I can be your son."

"You're my adopted son."

"Ohhh!" he exclaimed happily.

He remembered things in waves. His joints were covered in a wet orange fur. There was a humpback day moon in the sky mimicking his shape. Kafka was born long before the fall of the Coral Curtain, and came to us on the tides.

"I know what you're thinking!"

"Who took the car?" I ask aloud.

Strange physics: Kafka cannot lie. And that tail. Don't imagine a stuffed animal. What child would want to be a horseshoe crab? Appalling, the out of body experiences suffered by my son. His name-bird, a great collector, had abandoned him, or rather, actually tried to eat him. Time for Kafka was like the glass eye of a doll.

We walked along the beach. At the edge of the sea I noticed the shore birds had made the same tracks in the sand as my son.

THE LAST FISH

Harry Greatorex

The boy scampers ahead, bouncing from side to side down the old dirt track. The old man follows behind, the sun on his back seeping through his thin cotton shirt. He hurries now and then to keep the boy in sight, leaning on his good hip and swinging one leg around in a slow arc.

To the left, tall rubber trees reach overhead, moving softly and whispering in the breeze that rolls down sleepy hills to the West. As their branches swing and bow, the tiny shadows cast by their leaves scurry like small creatures over the bare earth, darting between patches of scrub faster than the eye can follow. To the right, the bank falls away to where the river winds heavy and slow. Here and there, floating logs caught up in the current provide makeshift boats for white-throated dacnis. They nip and pluck at the dried bark, dislodging grubs. They are tracked by what might be the ripples of water snakes – or might just be ripples.

"Go careful, *hijito*" the old man calls. He pauses and squints in the sunshine as the boy disappears around the bend in the path ahead. The old man leans his weight on a familiar branch that juts out in greeting. The bark is worn smooth just *here* where many tired hands have leaned before. And of these hands that pass this way no more, how many toil now, somewhere far beyond those hills? Hands that grasp shovel and sieve, deep under dusty towns sprung up from whispers of gold and tin. Those towns that heave with broken men and tired trucks and yet more men and more trucks.

By the time he reaches the river, the boy is unfurling his line at the edge of the water. His small hands work quickly. He checks for kinks and knots, removing a twig here, a tangle there. The old man sits in the shade to catch his breath. He watches as the boy goes about his work with keen eyes and nimble fingers.

"Not too deep," calls the old man. The boy is up to his waist now, the bright red of his shorts darkened beneath the surface of the water. The fabric sticks to his thighs and washes this way and that. He strides and stumbles where the river bed rises and falls to meet the hard soles of small feet.

As the sun reaches its highest point overhead and makes its first dip back towards the earth, the old man's chin meets his chest. Gentle snores drift across the water to where the boy squats, motionless, on a rock. He is lost in concentration as his line stretches its way to pierce the shadows beneath.

The boy shouts out and the old man stirs. He looks up to see the line fizzing through the water at the boy's ankles. The boy shouts again, louder – that high-pitched voice of half joy, half fear.

"Hold him, *hijito*! *Epa!*" the old man calls out.

The boy slips on the rock. Green moss squelches between his toes as he goes down, under the water then up, up again coughing and spluttering. The line fizzes past again, tightening around the boy's fingers.

"*Abuelo!*" he cries. "*Ya lo tengo* – I have him.*"

The fish thrashes to the surface. A plume of water bursts into the air, spattering the boy's face and chest.

The old man is on his feet now, pacing the river's edge. His hands are held aloft, empty fists opening and closing. His feet move together, the old hip forgotten. He sends up a cheer.

The boy reels his catch in, hand over hand. The fish comes up, up again, dancing across the shining surface of the water, then pulling deep below and out of sight. The line sings in the boy's hands. His eyes shine, his voice softened as he talks to the fish. Closer, closer. Now the single, wide eye of the fish. Now the cold of scales.

The boy splashes to the bank with his prize and finds a flat rock. Already the knife is in his hand. He works quickly, feeling the fish's life ebb away between his fingers.

The old man makes his way down the bank, his slow, swinging gait returned. A smile draws deep lines across his face.

The boy cries out. The old man pauses.

The boy bursts into tears. He draws back from the fish. A wailing echoes up and down the bank, drowning out the sound of the river.

By the time the old man reaches him, the boy's face is streaked. The rock is covered with droplets of river water that mingle with the tears as they fall. The old man clicks his tongue. He is never sure what to do about these things. After a moment, he takes hold of the boy. He is stiff in the old man's arms. Fresh tears pool on the thin cotton shirtfront.

"There, there, *hijito*. Whatever is the matter? Just look at this beautiful fish you have landed!"

The boy is talking now – a low mutter almost to himself. *What is that he is saying?*

"But I *like* school, *Abuelo*. I like Señora Martinez. And sitting next to Carmen. I like reading. And football. And I like José, and Danilo."

The old man shakes his head. "But of course you do! So what?"

The boy just shakes his head. The old man pauses for a second. He sees how the boy leans away from the fish. Now fear clutches a cold fist around the old man's stomach.

"Give it here."

"Don't look!"

The old man takes the fish into his own hands – cold of scale, wide of eye. He peers inside.

"*Abuelo*, don't look!"

There, between his fingers, all is as it should be: Red of blood, pink and purple of heart and lungs, white of bone, the raw hew of flesh. But then, in the river mud in the guts of the fish... something shining, glittering, golden. Where gold and glitter ought not to be.

"Don't!"

The old man leans in closer. *There.*

He catches his breath. He lets go of the boy and stands. He staggers two paces and slumps down on the broken stump of a tree. The boy watches him.

The old man shakes his head. "I've worked hard all my life," he says, his voice low. "I put up with the old man for twenty three years. I built my business up. Nothing beyond my means. I worked my fingers to the bone."

The boy watches, his cries subsiding.

"I took care to learn my trade. And to be an honourable man. I grew my family from two to three, to four, to many more."

The old man starts to sob, his shoulders heaving silently under his thin cotton shirt. The tiny shadows scurry around their feet like small creatures over the bare earth, darting between patches of scrub faster than the eye can follow. The boy puts a hand on the old man's shoulder.

LUCID

DM Tomkins

The only way to get through this is by dreaming. Matthew's had months to perfect his technique. Lucid dreams take him where he wants to be. He's in control.

Except.

Three nights into the journey, for instance. In his dream he'd chosen to be at the pub with friends. He walked in, happy and expectant, looking forward to a pie and a pint. What greeted him were charred and blackened ruins, skeletons, death.

He turned back to the city, tried to reset his dream, but was engulfed by a wall of fire sweeping towards him. He woke screaming.

No dream, this. A memory.

It happens more often, almost every night. If there are nights on a spaceship where you're the only conscious being.

Matthew experiments with shorter sleep periods, longer: four hours on, four off. Eight, sixteen, two. Sleeping pills, stimulants, videos, books. Nothing works.

People invade his dreams. His mother, his brothers, his baby sister. He promises their dream selves he'll make it, he'll send money home, he'll fetch them soon. They weep in his arms, make their farewells, embrace him for the last time. He tries desperately to reset, to see Earth blue and green as she once was. In his dreams he attempts a Martian reunion, his family stepping off the ship, ready to take their places as citizens of the terraformed planet.

By day, Matthew walks the ship's corridors, staring into the stasis pods. These contain people who paid more than him.

The captain quit before take-off. He left Matthew in charge, told him it was easy, the computer would do everything, and anyway, what did he expect for only half a million?

Now the computer tells him there's not enough energy to keep all five hundred alive. It asks him which half to jettison.

Matthew feels sick. He's seen bodies tumbling in space, some unbearably tiny. He presses the button, hopes he can get the rest to Mars. He's only nineteen.

A month later he rations his water. Then his food. There was never enough. He reduces the ship's energy to basic life-support but has to throw out the remaining passengers three weeks before touchdown.

He arrives on Mars skeletal and unable to stand, even under gravity lighter than Earth's. His hair has fallen out.

Matthew's arrested for murder. His counsel suggests a plea of insanity may be viewed favourably. A secure psychiatric facility would surely be better than life imprisonment, she says.

People with banners protest outside the courtroom in the thin Martian air and the pale Martian sunlight, stirring up the red Martian dust that stains everything. The banner people want an end to trafficking. They say it's unacceptable that thousands die every year making the hazardous journey in unsafe and illegal vessels. Matthew's not a criminal, they say, he's a victim.

Under the pink sky, Matthew sees trees and a vivid patchwork of green stretching to the horizon.

This is what he dreamt of. This is what he came for.

A WASH OF PURPLE

Emily Tremmis

Shona finds her on a Sunday night, so late it's early, splashing barefoot through the wavelets under the pier where she's not supposed to be. The mermaid – because what else can she be, long black hair and periwinkle scales on her tail – lies half-buried in sand, well above the water line, and when Shona tries to help her back into the waves, she screams, high and agonised, sharp enough to ring Shona's fillings.

Shona goes back the next night, sure that she dreamed the woman, but not so sure that she doesn't take a bucket with her when she goes.

The mermaid isn't a dream, and when Shona pours a slow stream of sea water over her, she trills in happiness, her scales rippling with the sound.

When Shona leaves, dawn is starting to paint the horizon, and she'd swear that the mermaid's scales have darkened to a soft lavender.

Tuesday night, Shona takes sushi with her, because what else can a mermaid eat under the waves?

Her mermaid turns her nose up at it, and when Shona holds some to her lips, she just looks back, dark eyes fixed on Shona like she can't be trusted.

"It's good," Shona promises. She's still surprised when the mermaid takes the mouthful from her fingers, but maybe not as surprised as her mermaid's face as she chews.

"Told you," Shona says, and takes more when she slips under the pier on Wednesday night, just as twilight is falling.

Maybe it's the changing light, but she thinks her mermaid's scales have darkened again, smoky heather like the hills where Shona was born.

Friday night, she combs sand from her mermaid's hair and wonders: what would happen if Shona kissed her? Would Shona grow a tail of her own, and dive away with her beneath the waves? Would her mermaid grow her own legs, and follow Shona back to the studio she shares with her cat?

Which would she want? Which would be worse?

What if nothing happened at all?

What if nothing happened at all, except that her mermaid kissed her back?

Her mermaid's scales are deep mauve, like the night.

And then, on Saturday night, Shona finds her mermaid waiting in the surf, waves breaking over scales the darkest amethyst that Shona has ever seen.

"Don't go," she says.

Her mermaid trills in response, hair a cloud around her as the waves take her further away.

"Please," Shona says.

Her mermaid smiles, soft and mournful.

Before Shona can ask again, she flips her tail, and disappears beneath the waves.

It takes Shona two weeks to go back, ruthlessly crushing the part of her that hopes she'll find her mermaid waiting for her when she does.

There's no-one, of course, and she's turning to leave, blinking away tears, when the glint of moonlight against glass catches her eye.

Hanging from a nail she's never before noticed in the support for the pier, barely above the water line, is a string of shells, polished to the highest shine, and in the very centre of the string, a perfect round amethyst, the exact same colour as her mermaid's scales.

She folds her hands around it, trapping the unexpected warmth of the stone, and for a moment, she's sure that she hears the lilting trill of her mermaid's voice when she was happy.

Ten years later, every Sunday evening, so late it could be early, Shona still goes splashing barefoot through the wavelets under the pier where she's not supposed to be.

There's never a mermaid there again, but she stands in the surf, hand pressed to the amethyst in the centre of the necklace she never takes off, and looks out to the sea, listens through the waves, and lets herself believe that the shimmer of purple, the high trill of an unseen voice, is her mermaid, letting her know that she's never alone.

ORIGAMI DREAMS

Alexander MJ Smith

Paper wings, coaxed out of paper bodies by nothing but practice and patience.

My grandmother taught me origami, between strawberry daifuku and arguments with Mum. She'd learned it from her own mother while they reeled from the Allied firebombs, and now I feel those years guiding my fingers as I fold.

Ridges and furrows; in me, in the paper. Our origins working together.

But despite my aunt and uncle's promises, washi paper is hard to find in this foreigner's city. As is quiet. I'm making do with the paper they've bought, treating its inferiority as just another challenge. As for the inescapable noise, I hope I'll become accustomed with time.

How much time? I can't imagine.

And so tonight, like every night since I arrived, I'm making dreams for people. Folding instead of sleeping because I couldn't if I tried, while my cousin's easy snores remind me that sooner or later I'll have to accept this place as home.

I'd hoped the repetition would lull me; maybe nostalgia would fuzz up and send me off. But instead the potential of my creations rattles through me, insomnious nights are given purpose, and I imbue the paper with spritzing promise in every crease, all the while loving and arguing with the absent women who taught me how.

When the dreams are ready, I'll push them into the space between this building and the next. Most will spiral down to the street and wait, flattened and sodden, to be pulped by the morning traffic. Others will be intercepted by real birds, who eat paper ones for fun.

But some – maybe even just one – will dance on the thermals to cross the gap and venture out into this strange city, taking it in and checking it's safe, before drifting through open windows to touch down beside sleeping heads.

For now they're lined up on the windowsill. One for every window.

THEME AND VARIATIONS

Alice Little

I was born, if we can call it that, in Paris, circa 1889. I can't be precise because in the workshop individual pieces might be left for some time before being assembled into a violin.

My first owner was a music student at the Conservatoire. He came from a prominent Russian family, and he took me back east when he finished his studies. Sometimes we played classical music, but I preferred the nights spent playing Klezmer for his friends to dance to, stamping their feet and clapping their hands, swirling scarves and laughing together. I took several knocks at crowded gatherings, but I was young and it didn't seem to matter.

At the turn of the century, when he had children of his own I was passed to his son. The boy had soft fingers, but eventually we mastered his exercises. When the son grew up he took me west once more, to Berlin: a city broken after the Great War, where the winters were nearly as cold as in Russia. There he became a mathematics professor, performing at weekends for his friends, but we didn't play the old tunes any more.

The professor's own son was only twelve when I was passed down to the next generation, on the eve of a new war. The boy had barely started learning to play, but his shoulders were strong and he had confidence. I had never been held like that before.

We left Berlin suddenly, crushed among children on a noisy train. Having crossed the North Sea we were stopped by an official who thought the boy planned to sell me for cash upon arrival in England. I was stunned by the very idea: was I not his own violin, a tangible connection to his Russian grandfather, something familiar to hold in his new life far from home?

"His parents gave him the violin because he likes to play," our escort said, standing at the head of a queue of children, in front of the British customs officers.

"Play then," a guard said brusquely.

The boy lifted me to his shoulder and bowed the strings. I sang as sweetly as I could, trying to help prove he could play. Then, recognising the tune, I switched to a bold, strong tone. The guards stood to attention. The tune was God Save the King. We played three verses. They let us pass.

We saw out the war as peacefully as we could, and I went with the boy afterwards when he found work on a farm in Cambridgeshire. We didn't play much: I suppose he only kept me because I'd been given to him by his father. I lay dejectedly in my wooden case for many years, wrapped in my old silk scarf. I didn't like the dampness of the seasons in England but over the years I adjusted and no harm was done. The boy – no longer a boy – lived another forty years, and when he died I was sold to an antiques shop, my strings rusted and broken but otherwise I was still in good condition.

I next belonged to a young French academic who liked the thought of playing the violin more than the realities of practice. She collected beautiful things and spotted me as soon as I went on display in the shop. She saw that my maker's label was Parisian, like herself, and did not guess that in fact I spoke many languages.

I spent the university terms lounging on top of her piano: her friends would play sonatas with me when they came over for tea. She knew about instruments and kept me in good condition for her friends, but it wasn't the same as being with one person, developing a rapport. I longingly recalled the intense Russian tunes, the soft fingers of the professor, and even that brave anthem of the boy, short-lived though the moment had been.

The young French academic gained her doctorate, and stayed in Cambridge to work in a museum. She died suddenly in middle age, and her relatives donated all her instruments to the museum's collection.

My bow was taken away for a special exhibition, and I was shut in my old-fashioned case on a high shelf in the storeroom: not rare enough to be of interest to researchers, but old enough to be worth preserving. I was occasionally lent to students when their own instruments were out for repairs, but it was a quiet life.

Then just last week I found myself on the move again, this time heading to Turkey, where I had been promised to a teenager. The boy had left his home in a hurry and, arriving in a new town with no school to attend, no books to read, and nothing better to do, he had taken up playing the violin: teaching himself from online videos, using a beaten-up instrument he had found by chance.

The museum in Cambridge, hearing his story, had sought out a decent instrument to send to him: one that wasn't too valuable, but good enough for a serious student of music. Little did they know that this was the sort of work I had become accustomed to, the sort of journey I had been making all my life.

First I was spruced up, a bow was found, and I was placed in a special protective case. Then – a strange sensation – we flew south, to a place I had never been before, where the air is dry and the music is wild.

The boy's hands are rough, but he has strong fingers and knows how to make a melody dance. He has written a number of tunes especially for me, and we join in with songs on the radio: he can't sing along, he doesn't understand the words.

So here I am, over a century old, still travelling the world and learning new music. And though our current home is only temporary, I have found my own new home with him.

A SHORT HISTORY OF COAT-GIVING

Gavin Ritchie

Tariq hasn't spoken yet, and he won't hold my hand crossing dangerous roads. I'm told it takes time. When I talk to him it is slow, deliberate, and elementary; I wonder if he thinks English isn't swift enough to hold in its hands the terrible beauty or the vertiginous anguish Arabic can. As for crossing roads, we're all right. We are.

Tariq means 'he who pounds on the door.' I looked it up. Funny I should remember it now. He who pounds on the door. I imagined something more divine, to be honest, but now, well, he suits it.

The word spatula confused him. He knew bullet, though. His confused little face; his frown. He stood there in the coat he's so far refused to take off. Even through the night, when he slept; it had to be next to him[1]. I pointed out, in the kitchen, that the bullet was for juicing vegetables and that it was just called bullet because, well, never mind, I said. There are places, places in his memory, I really didn't want to go. Then I started misplacing things.

---

[1] In her seminal anthropological text, *Humanity's Anomia: Struggling with Angels* (Chicago: Labyrinth Press, 1989), Professor Jamieson Twigg catalogues the fourteen ritualistic functions of coat-giving:

    a.   Coats given as rites of passage,
    b.   Coats given as means of disguise,
    c.   Coats given for the purpose of collecting bullet casings,
    d.   Coats given as emblems of faith,
    e.   Coats given as much in jealousy as in love,
    f.   Coats given at three minutes past the hour,
    g.   Coats given as a means of identification in a crowd, or at a distance,
    h.   Coats given by strangers,
    i.   Coats given for no reason at all,
    j.   Coats given because the men in the room are greatly stressed,
    k.   Coats given in the reigning theoretical paradigms and all the paradigms yet to be named,
    l.   Coats given for expressed reasons, e.g. because you're shivering, because you don't look well,
    m. Coats given then quickly taken back,
    n.   Coats given while a couple scream at each other because their daughter is missing

So, I decided: we'd go to the park.

I felt the way you do when you carry something precious outside the first time, something you've got to keep safe, something so prized in the world it shines and everyone sees it, can see you're holding it close and they want it for themselves and the only reason they wouldn't dream of taking it is they can see it shine in your face, too, and it'd be a horror to separate you from it and if they did they'd never be human again.

People looked at me; they stared at Tariq in his big coat. It covered his knees. Every now and then, he'd bury his nose in the wool collar; he'd press the dark, long sleeve into his cheek. When he went into his little bubble, he wouldn't hear me; I just had to let him get over it, get through it.

Tariq tells me he understands a word by pointing at my mouth and then at his temple. The way he does it, I picture my words vanishing into his little head. He does this a lot more for concrete things than for abstract words, like yesterday, age, war. We do a lot of pointing.

The ice cream van, the trees, the birds, all fascinated Tariq. I pointed; he pointed. I said van, squirrel, sycamore, silver birch, pigeon.

Tariq looked at the object, at my mouth, and took the word, the thing, in with his fierce dark eyes. He'd follow my finger to the tree, to its bark, its height, its leaves. He'd gaze at my lips when I'd say, for instance, silver birch. I'd say it again. Then, all magic - his finger emerging from his long coat sleeve, his pink finger end, a nubbin from the darkness – his brows would tighten, and he'd move his finger through the air, turning the word into a phantom he could pull across the gulf between us. It was as if he had silver birch in a tractor beam. He drew it across and sent it to live in his head.

The squirrel we saw was fast, was there one minute, gone the next. The ice cream van went off to somewhere new.

Once around the park, Tariq and I were back where we started. It looked the same as it had before, except for the silver birch. It wasn't there. I went closer, went right over to where it had been, where it had always been. The ground was undisturbed. The council hadn't come and pulled the tree out, I thought. Why would they?

It bothered me for a minute.

At the main road again, daylight dying, the traffic was louder, angrier, its impatience had grown. Tariq, love, I said, Tariq? I showed him my hand. I asked him nicely and he smiled, but he kept his hands in the pockets of his coat. His smile was one of those where the eyes faint together, all apology. He stood closer to me so his shoulder bumped into my leg.

When we crossed the road, I put an arm around him, resting a hand on his other shoulder. I felt shielded from the traffic.

My house was dark, empty; I pointed, home, I said. Tariq's stare softened when he put it inside his head. He was still leaning into me when I slid the key into the door. Nothing turned; I must have locked us out. So, I phoned for help – it's what we do here – then took Tariq back to the park, where we stayed a while.

We lay on the grass next to the place where the silver birch had been and gaped at the stars. The cosmos twitched on a knife-edge. Stars faded; most came back.

Neither of us said a word.

THERE WAS HOPE

Tess Clare Lily

Tarajjā touched her hands to her face to remind herself of the space between her mouth, nose, eyes, and cheeks. She hadn't seen her reflection for a long time and now she was outside all day, there were no mirrors.

She didn't want to go too close to the cars because they always beeped loudly and they frightened her, but she thought that she might be able to see her reflection if the sun was at the right point in the sky.

She wondered if her eyes were still brown. Every time she closed them, she felt the motion of the boat bobbing up and down, so she tried to keep them open as long as she could. Sometimes she would yawn ten times before she fell asleep.

In the mornings, the sun woke her up very early but she enjoyed listening to the birds. They sang bright songs and she sang back.

Tarajjā spoke to them too, and although she knew they couldn't really understand her, she liked to think that some of them might have been in the skies near her old house. After all, birds could go from one side of the world to another without going in a boat or a van because they could fly.

Ever since the trip on the boat, her mother coughed a lot. She said she was very cold. She cried too, especially when Tarajjā asked about her little brother, Aimar. Her Mum would say that he was with Tarajjā's uncle, but she knew that must be a fib because Aimar came on the boat with them and her uncle did not.

Tarajjā missed Aimar the most. He could walk but he would sometimes fall over when he tried to run, so she held his hand whenever they were in a rush. Some of the men who helped them over the seas were worried that Aimar might cry out and be too loud, but he was a good boy and never made a sound.

If he was with her now, Tarajjā would give him a big squeeze and tell him he was going to grow up big and strong.

Her father was already in the UK, he had made the trip a few months before, but they couldn't find him now.

One day, some people in uniforms came to their camp and asked lots of questions, wrote down everyone's names and took some people's temperatures with a thermometer.

She hid in her tent whilst they walked around. Her heart was beating very loudly when they opened the tent up to look inside. When they found her, they gave each other lots of frowned looks and spoke in muffled tones.

Tarajjā thought they were a bit strange.

They came back to the camp lots of times after that. They often brought supplies and shared them out between as many people as they could, but there was never enough for everyone.

Sometimes they took people away from the camp. Tarajjā didn't know where they went, but they never came back.

One morning, they came straight to Tarajjā's tent to talk with her and her mother. They explained that they wanted to introduce them to a lady called Mrs. Clare and that she was going to help.

They walked Tarajjā through the camp and took her to a car. At first, she thought she saw a girl inside, but it was her own reflection. She smiled. The sun must have been at the right point in the sky.

As they drove away, she stared out of the window and imagined she was a horse, running as fast as she could across the fields.

When they arrived, they sat her in a small room with a table and two chairs and then Mrs. Clare walked in.

"Hello, how are you?" said Mrs. Clare.

"Hello, Mrs. Clare," she replied, in her best English.

Mrs. Clare had blonde hair and blue eyes with a kind face. "Call me Olivia," she said, "and I'll call you Tarajjā. Is that okay?"

Tarajjā nodded and brushed her hair behind her ear. She wanted to look presentable in front of her new friend.

"Have they explained to you why I'm here?" Olivia asked.

Tarajjā shook her head with her mouth closed. She was afraid to speak too much English in case she got her words muddled up.

"I'm going to bring you to my village, where we will make sure you have a nice place to live, with tasty food and warm clothes and everything you need," Olivia said.

Tarajjā nodded. That was very kind.

"There are lots of people who want to make sure you have a brilliant life, Tarajjā. We will help you in every way that we can," Olivia continued.

"And Aimar?" Tarajjā asked.

There was a long pause.

"I'm sorry, Tarajjā. We won't be able to bring Aimar. He has gone to heaven now," Olivia spoke slowly, she wasn't smiling now.

Tarajjā thought of her little brother and then thought of her dad. "What about Father?" she said.

"We're still looking for him, Tarajjā, but I promise we won't give up," said Olivia.

Tarajjā felt her face getting hot and her eyes filling with tears, "Please don't take me away from my Mum," Tarajjā whispered. "Let me stay with her."

Olivia reached over and took hold of Tarajjā's hand, "We're going to help you and your Mum too," she said. "We'll help you say goodbye to Aimar and we'll keep looking for your dad. We know his name and where he was living. He's probably looking for you too."

"After I say goodbye to Aimar and after we find my dad, can I go to school and learn about the world?" Tarajjā asked and Olivia nodded. "Can I sing like the birds? And can I run like the horses?" Tarajjā asked.

Olivia nodded again and smiled this time, "You can do all of those things and more," she said.

Tarajjā smiled too. For the first time since the boat trip, she was excited for tomorrow. There was hope.

GYRE

Marc Nash

Bodies on display in the street. Burst pipes spewed clean water and dirty sewage like impromptu fountains. I stood at the lip of the crater where my parents' home once stood. I didn't know if they were dead or had just fled. Either way it amounted to the same outcome. We were asunder for good. There was nothing keeping me here, but plenty to propel me away.

I headed west, among a gaggle of others. Some stopped and turned around to pray in the direction we were forsaking. Otherwise, they didn't bother to look back. They weren't praying for a return to their homeland. For the rest of us, our new god faced the other way. We honoured the sun setting on our lives by making a headlong pilgrimage accelerating our progress there.

As more joined our throng, we felt like a drove prodded by an unseen goatherd. I couldn't see a bell around my neck alerting them to our presence, yet wranglers eyed us suspiciously at the border. They branded us with their marks on our papers yet would not let us stay on as their property. They marched us past ranks of policemen stood in front of shuddering chain-link fences as the locals slapped the wire and screamed at us through the mesh. We were put in a temporary camp at their other border, where we were now the ones contained behind metal, the fingers of the adults blanched bloodless so tight did they grip the mesh, while us children's wrists were able to slip through the chinks as we wrung our hands nervously. Yet we were missing the third limb, that of the police to protect us from predations by others within the wire.

We moved on. Hanging from trains or 4x4s like creeping vines, though some of us human berries dropped off and were crushed underfoot, or were threshed by non-fruit pickers. Whether juice, pulp or seed, the ferment in our wake meant we could not lay down roots here.

And on we trudged. Overhead a flock of geese, their tight formation presented them as a fleet of military aircraft, or perhaps their array of freshly released bombs. The child next to me threw himself to the ground. No one helped him up. The aerial migrators glided unerringly straight while we ploddingly snaked, their voyage smooth since they were never challenged for their papers. They were ebulliently raucous where we were bone-wearily silent. They flew perpendicularly over us and I contemplated adopting their direction from latitude to longitude. But I could not raise my feet high enough to escape the rut in the sand that our human train had pressed.

We reached the coast and found that the sea would always welcome us with open arms into its bosom. It would always have berths for us to lay down and never rise again. Packed into boats like sardines, once the boat was tipped up and emptied, we scattered and were spread out on the waves. The boats sunk but we floated bloated. Until we were hooked like a fish at a funfair (that too would only live for the shortest time), or we finally settled on land, buried beneath its soil.

In Europe, as we were passed from pillar to post, or rather temporarily lashed one from the other, I thought of the Wandering Jew. Supposedly our mortal enemy, now we walked in his exact footsteps. Had he closed the way for us several centuries later? He, of course, had the advantage of being a shoemaker who could thus repair his own leather, where our callused and bloodied hooves were not so fortunate. Our feet aped that of the European messiah where nails had been driven in to tether him to his pillar and post. The natives do not offer us such sympathy, devotion or care. Instead they hit us, shouted at us to pick up our lacerated feet quicker.

And so we do. We get the same reception in every country we cross into. Which is to say no reception at all, we are not received in the slightest. We are like the interference on TV screens, the white noise on the wireless. With which one turn of the dial, they tune us out and restore their home broadcasts.

Eventually we wash back up on the shores of our original homeland. We have traversed the earth seeking sanctuary.

And now our levelled home ringed with fire and bullets, our fellow countrymen are rounded up and compacted like shawarma meat on the rotisserie before a giant knife comes and slices off the outer layers. Still more inviting than the treatment we received at the closed hands of our fellow man.

OVER THE BORDER

Mike Evis

The border had to be close now. Could it be behind the dark woods we were walking towards, or was it over the hills beyond? Whichever it was, it wasn't far now. We were going to make it, thank God.

Except... something wasn't right. I paused, and the others looked round at me. The shadows between the trees were moving. That was odd...

"No!" I shouted as the shadows became figures; soldiers advancing from the trees, rifles trained on us. "No!" This was so unfair. We were so close.

I raised my hands, wondering why I bothered. What did it matter? Once I couldn't imagine the army would shoot at its own people – but that was before the demonstration. So I stood, frozen to the spot, waiting for the firing to start, but in my mind I was back there in the square, remembering the screams, the groans, the blood, so much blood, and the endless gunfire. I should have died too that day. It had been futile to escape, to come all this way, I should have accepted my fate. Now it had caught up with me.

See, I was never political, never interested in the news. Bored me rigid. Jacob was the one who came back, night after night, saying "Have you heard what they've done now, Alana?" and I'd look up, uninterested, and unwilling to drag myself away from my paperback, muttering, "Who cares?"

Then he'd get annoyed and grab me by the shoulders, saying I shouldn't be like that, insisting there were things worth fighting for – freedom, democracy – "Yeah, sure," I'd mutter, anything to get rid of him. I learned to agree in the end, it was easier. I would dart an occasional quick look across at my book, reading odd words and sentences until he left me alone and I could read properly again.

I remember the day he came back, excitedly going on and on about the long lines of army lorries filled with soldiers he'd seen parked on the streets outside government offices.

"They're planning something," he said.

"Don't be so silly," I said, throwing my paperback wearily onto the table. I was irritated, I'd nearly reached the end, and soon everything was going to be revealed. I had to read on. "It's just an exercise," I sighed. "That's all. You're paranoid, you really are."

"They took my boss away earlier."

"What? But – he's always been a hothead, you said that yourself."

"You don't see, do you? New laws, rounding up people – soon it'll be a dictatorship."

"Just listen to yourself. Will you just listen to yourself sometimes?"

But I was the one who should have listened.

"There's a big demo planned tomorrow. We have to go."

"It won't achieve anything,' I said. 'Waste of time. And what if it turns violent?'"

"It won't. It's a peaceful demonstration."

In the end, I agreed to go. I knew he'd only go without me otherwise, and then he'd stagger back at midnight, full of beer, talking about the activists he'd met in the pub, the fascinating conversations they'd had, the plans they'd made, and by the end it would be two am before I'd get any sleep.

Tears ran down my face as I recalled the deceptive sunshine that morning, the vast crowds, the banners waving in the breeze, the impassioned speeches – and then the soldiers lined up around the edge of the square. The sound of what I thought were firecrackers, the sudden panic as someone shouted 'That's live fire!', the screams of people running in terror, and the endless shooting. I crouched, as the shots ricochetted around me behind a statue rapidly becoming bullet ridden, praying for it to end. But the silence that came – I never want to hear anything like that ever again. Nor do I want to smell the fear and death that drifted over the square like the acrid smoke in the air. A solitary cry broke that awful silence. "Murder! Murderers!" It was cut short by a few further shots.

Instinct made me run. I hated myself for leaving him there, amidst the dead and the dying, but I knew as I gulped back burning tears that he was gone. The first shots caught him; how they missed me I'll never know. I wish they'd taken me too. It was all over so fast. A sharp crack, his body jerking as if pulled on a wire, his eyes flickering and then he was still, as that awful pool of redness spread and spread over the flagstones. That was it. I heard the soldiers laughing and joking – "this'll teach them" – amidst the frantic calls of the injured and the dying.

I came back to the present. Five soldiers surrounded us. Another one, an officer, strolled over.

"Refugees?" he said.

We nodded, unwillingly, like children asked to admit wrongdoing, knowing what was coming.

"Lower your rifles, lads," he said.

"You're safe," he said. "You're not in England any more. You're over the border. You've reached the Scottish Republic."

THE PAST IS YOURS

Mike Evis

I don't know what I'll do if I can't visit the Thirties again. See, I was born in the wrong era. I'd rather be living in simpler times, before everything went crazy and got so messed up. To be alive in a time before terrorism, nuclear weapons and looming environmental disaster – don't you long for that too? Stuck here in the twenty first century, with no escape, it's like hell on earth.

It was pure chance when I picked up some sheets from an old newspaper as they blew along the pavement one morning. What caught my eye was the advert on one of the crumpled pages: 'Visit the Time Portal'. Intrigued, I read on, and when I saw the phrases 'To travel in time' and 'Visit the 30s', I knew this was it. This was what I'd been looking for all my life. 'The past is yours!' it read and that was more than enough for me.

For a few hours I can get away, to a pub in Thirties London, and forget about all the horrors of our modern age. I'm a refugee back in another time before everything became so complicated and perplexing. There's no one standing at the brown stained wood of the bar bellowing into their mobile phone, or worse, staring wordlessly at its screen all night. There's no fifty inch TV endlessly showing the latest disasters on the 24 hour news channel, or blaring out sports results. And no monotonous music pounding relentlessly in your ear, drowning out conversation.

When I walk in, Harry the barman, greets me with a weary smile. "How are you, Tim? Usual, is it?"And I nod to the regulars as I hand over a few coppers. I'm careful now to check my pockets each time, remembering the faux pas on my second or third visit when I forgot and handed over modern coins by mistake. I knew at once what I'd done from the shock on Harry's face, as he discreetly leant over the bar.

"Sorry, sir – have you've been overseas?"

I fumbled in my pocket, red faced.

"Don't worry, sir – I'll put it on your tab," he said.

I was lucky he didn't throw me out.

But, assuming I don't repeat my mistake, I taste a warm beer like no one in the twenty first century has tasted in a long, long time.

"Have one yourself, Harry," I say.

"Why, you're a gent, sir, don't mind if I do."

Then I walk over and sit down with the regulars to join in a game of cards. There's no talk of politics or the looming threat of war. It's just far enough back in the Thirties that trouble with Germany can still be shrugged aside. Like I say, simple, uncomplicated times.

So imagine my horror one week when I went through the Portal on my way to the Thirties – only to find I was somewhere else entirely. It might still have been the Thirties, but I wasn't in London, I was in a Berlin nightclub, towards the end of the Weimar Republic.

How had this happened? Funnily enough, the barman looked just like Harry. This was half a continent away, yet he was a complete dead ringer. He could have been a twin. But his eyes were blank, showing no sign he knew me.

"Harry," I said. "What's going on?" His eyes narrowed.

"Was ist das?"

"Where is – this is wrong, surely I should be in London?"

"Ich verstehe sie nicht."

"Come off it, Harry, what is this?"

"Ah – Englische," he smiled, shaking his head, and I noticed two men with swastika armbands look round, taking a sudden interest. I didn't hang around. Something was badly wrong and I wanted out of there. Even the present day was better than this.

I was nervous the next time I went through, but to my relief, everything was back to normal. Harry wasn't German, and I was back in the familiar London pub I knew.

"Last week-" I said to Harry.

"I'm sorry about that, sir. Couldn't be helped, what with the cellar all flooded."

"Oh – I see. But it's all right now?"

"Oh yes, sir. We only had to shut that one day."

But lately there don't seem to be so many regulars. Sometimes there aren't even enough for a game of cards. And one night I went in and there was just me and Harry there. Maybe they're all driving out to these new places that are springing up in the suburbs.

Then the worst happened, last week. Harry sidled up to me, whilst he was picking up glasses, and said, "I'm sorry to tell you this, sir, you being a regular and all, but I've got some bad news. The place is closing down at the end of the month."

"What? But why?"

He shrugged.

"Just not the trade there used to be. Not the demand for this sort of place."

"That's a real shame – I like it here. But what's going to happen?"

He shrugged.

"Have to move with the times, sir. The Sixties – now that's become really popular – all those baby boomers I expect. The Fifties too – that's been drawing a good crowd. You could try one of those."

"They're not really my period."

"No. Well, there's always Thirties Berlin. They're keeping that going."

"Too many Nazis," I said.

"That's the Weimar Republic for you," he said. "I'm none too keen on it myself but it pays the bills."

I remembered straightening out the newspaper to read the original ad in full.

'Visit the Time Portal – To travel in time may be impossible – but with our range of theme nights you can do the next best thing – Visit the 30s and drink at a genuine London pub of the period; Boogie the night away at a 70s disco; Get sorted for Es at a 90s rave. And lots more. The past is yours!'

THE ETERNAL REFUGEE

Mike Evis

Overcome with weariness, she sat down on the dusty trail that stretched off into the distance, unsure whether she would ever get up.

The desert was unforgiving and the others had all perished now – her mother last of all, but before that father, her twin brothers, her aunt and uncle, they'd all gone. Soon it would be her turn. It couldn't be long now. They had trudged for days across the hostile sands, till only she was left. And what for? For a hope that was as lacking as water. And soon her bottle would be empty and there would be no more. So far from home, so far from Europe, she thought, all our dreams over, abandoned in this desolate waste.

She must have dozed under the hot sun, for the next thing she knew the first stars were twinkling in the sky. Light -headed, in the rapidly fading daylight she thought she glimpsed other figures, on other trails, tramping across the empty sands.

A shadow fell across her face and she started. Someone stood over her, an old man smiling down, his hand stretched out towards her, saying something in a language she couldn't understand. Except at that instant, the words came into her mind: "You are not alone."

And she knew that the endless lines of people on the move stretched back not just across this desert here, but back across centuries, across tens of thousands of years, back into that deep time before there were even humans. It wasn't only into the past either. The columns on the march extended forwards far into the future.

Enthralled, she watched, as they wearily filed across unknown lands and continents, relentlessly on the move. Men, women, children, young, old, the persecuted, the restless, the dreamers, the explorers, victims of war, famine, natural disasters all before her. How could there be so many? But she began to understand that this had always been the way.

From her vantage point on the top of a sand dune, she watched them walking out of Africa, out of Eden, out of the Near East, across Europe, Asia, the Americas, setting sail across calm seas and wild oceans – never staying in one place, always moving, not always of their choice, yet other times simply feeling the call of the unknown.

And she wept. From sadness at her loss, and also from sadness at all their losses – for the tiny babies, the old and the sick who didn't make it – but also from the strange yet beautiful grandeur of it all, and the connection, the sense of unity with them all made across space and time.

The old man turned; he too could not stay, and repeated the same words. Again she understood them as "You are not alone", and she wept. The long weary procession of figures faded and became indistinct in the darkness, and she realised as they faded from view that she'd been granted a rare vision. There were millions upon millions like her. There had been millions more in the past. There would be millions more in the future. It would go on forever, as long as there were humans on Earth.

STOCKHOLM SYNDROME

Paul David Holland

One day, nearing his sixteenth birthday, he thought about how it might feel if he had woken up from a coma, just as his grandfather had suffered, as if he'd been asleep for ages, ten years, or even, let's say, twenty.

He grabbed his bike and raced out of the yard, into the street, past the beggars and the sellers, and into the main road that led past the temple, out of the Old Town.

When he reached the edge, he stopped and stood breathless, looking ahead. Through the distant, early-morning haze, the tower blocks loomed like giant robots, marching towards him.

He stared for longer than he normally would; he had never seen them like this before: personifications of malice making their relentless way into his world.

Not human, and not sentient, thoughtful, or sensitive – these were unblinking automata, soulless and unflinching as they advanced.

Cranes were attendant: vast metal structures working their way up tower block skeletons, slowly pecking their way up the flanks like real birds on the sides of great, lumbering beasts. Then gradually working down again, leaving behind the cladding that showed each new block was complete.

Wrong sort of cranes, he thought. His grandfather had described the farm pens and tumbledown outhouses that had littered this landscape before, the half-ruined temples, the tracks down to the river where black-necked cranes fished, the coming and going of peasants with their produce, the children running about half-naked. All this was now beneath the slick, smooth tarmac, the organised smartness that day by day is hardly noticed...

He climbed back on his bike and cycled further out to confront the giants lurching towards his family.

As he neared, he let his newly-woken self be astounded by their silence, compared with the sheer thundering noise all around him. Their quiescent nature close-up made them even more eerie, more threatening and sinister, while the clattering, chattering, honking clamour of the noisy streets swirled around their feet. When did it all become so loud? Had nobody noticed?

He cycled on through the straight streets: on past shops with glass fronts, plastic fascia boards; past specialists selling medicines, horn powder, antlers and the like; through wide plazas with nondescript monuments and statues to heroes whose names were in a different language; through shopping malls, pedestrian crossings, traffic lights, and traffic too, so much traffic; office blocks, apartment blocks, government blocks; then road blocks, police stations, sentry posts; and there, in full view, military patrols, marching along streets in formation, like the buildings around them, guns slung ostentatiously across their shoulders, with the soldier at the rear sporting a small fire-extinguisher.

Was this a part of his childish imagination or not?

He blinked, hoping to break the spell he had set. Hoping to unsee some of these things now, as if he could shake off the knowledge. But he could not.

His father had said: "Son, it's progress, let it be. Your grandfather couldn't stop it, I can't and you certainly won't, not now. It's gone too far. Look at it."

Now hospitals, roads, railways, airports, clean houses, clean streets, supermarkets, restaurants, tourists, bus-stations, bus-stops, parks, squares and shops, running water, drains, law and order... whatever we need we have. There's never been a better time to live here, so they say.

For what was here before? A desperate state, cocooned in a desolation almost tangible in its remoteness. Not even the ramshackle dereliction still found in parts of the Old Town can truly bring back to mind the horrors of the squalor, the destitute sadness, the poverty.

But it was our poverty, wasn't it? Nobody else's. Who'd want it, anyway?

'It's like we're refugees in our own home,' he'd once heard his grandfather say, the one who put himself to sleep for so long, and who had afterwards hardly been able to walk again, whose skin had burnt off and whose clouded eyes no longer had to look at unwanted progress.

Exile takes on some funny forms, thought the boy as he turned his bike back home.

And change doesn't always feel like change, not when it wants to shirk from the new, the modern, the crass, the endless waves of incomers, hungry for a share in it all.

On his way back, dodging cars and motorbikes, he tried to look at the Old Town too, with his new eyes, but his vision kept getting hidden by images of all the passers-by in flames. A protest too far, he thought, though the giants would certainly have the run of the whole place, if we all went up like that.

Stopping at the temple, he put his bike against the wall and went in. No imagination ever stole in here.

JOURNEY'S END

Diana Brighouse

You see me.

I can feel your eyes on me before I see you.

The road is slick with water, rivulets running down the potholed surface, my frayed trainers inadequate for the miles that I've walked. I can feel a small crack in one sole that is steadily eroding into a proper hole. Inside the shoe, my foot is wet. The woman in front of me has an umbrella, and I wonder how she got it, what she's had to sell. I have an old plastic bag tied around my head, which crackles when I move, and distorts what I hear. I don't know who I'm trying to keep my hair nice for – do I really believe that you'll be here?

When I said, all that time ago, that I'd follow you at the end of the semester, I never imagined it would end like this. Crammed into filthy trucks that smelled like public toilets, struggling through muddy fields in the dark, and always having to trust the sort of men I'd normally cross the road to avoid. Did you wonder if I'd get out? Did you think I'd give up, imagine the journey impossible for a woman travelling alone? But of course, I was never alone, though God knows there have been times when I wished I was.

Finally, I am here. Here on the wet, cold, dark streets, in the country whose language we started to learn. Ich komme aus Syrien. Ich bin Lehrer an der Universitat. They won't care that I teach in a university. To them, I'm just another faceless, nameless woman. Another anonymous person in dirty jeans and someone else's coat. Another person without passport or possessions. A refugee - how I hate that word.

As we turn the corner I see people waiting for us, their placards saying, 'Refugees Welcome.' There are ten or twelve of them, standing quietly, the rain dripping off their signs. They smile at us, but their smiles don't go past their lips. Behind them is an old building with huge, solid columns – a bank, maybe.

I think I see you, standing apart, in the shadow of a column. As we get nearer, I am certain that it is you.

I can set the terror and uncertainty behind me.

I look again, longing to bury my face in your chest, to smell you, to feel your arms tight around me.

You are gone.

*

I heard that another group was arriving this afternoon. It is a foul day, wet and cold; one of those days when it never gets light. In the early days I used to come every time, hoping that she had made it. I imagined her making arrangements to travel. That was before the news started to report how many people were desperate to travel, how many were dying on the journey to Europe.

Eventually I gave up hope. I grieved for her, for our life before the bombs. But I have to make my future here in my adopted country.

So now I come to the welcome group for a different reason. I have a girlfriend, and we are talking about marriage. She thinks I am a widower.

I see them, a group of about twenty or thirty straggling up the road. They all look the same in the gloom, shapeless and dejected. One or two have umbrellas, the only splashes of colour.

I watch the TV, but still I feel angry. How can my countrymen let themselves be so humiliated? The women look dirty, not proud. I finger the wool of my coat and glance at my sturdy shoes. I arrived here three years ago, by plane, the last foreign conference before the government clamped down. Conversations in the right places allowed me to claim political asylum. She was going to follow me at the end of the semester.

Then her university was bombed. I saw the newspapers, the television. I heard nothing.

Suddenly I see her. Shapeless, dirty and drab as the others, but her head, with her hair in a ridiculous plastic bag, is held high.

It is my wife.

For a second our eyes meet. A lifetime has passed since we last touched.

I melt into the shadows.

WHERE ARE MY SHOES?

Ruby Vallis

The man and the boy sit on big stones under one of the few trees on the desolated stretch of road, waiting for the bus. The boy distracts himself with a stick, stopping red ants from climbing on his toes. They both look into the distance when they hear rattling; they stand up ready. And, when the bus is nearer, the driver's assistant swings his body out of the door like a trapeze artist who is about to fall, and shouts, "Cartagena! Cartagena, one thousand pesos!"

"Do you go to the terminal?" the man asks. The bus slows down.

"Yes, jump on."

"It's only the boy, Aldemar," the man says, and at the same time the man lifts the boy into the bus.

"A woman called Oliva will be waiting for him," the man tells the driver.

"Papa, I don't want to go."

The man takes a pair of shoes from a bag and hands them to him, 'For your first communion,' he says. The bus moves faster. The boy's eyes redden.

"Cartagena! Cartagena Terminal!" The assistant shouts again but there is no one around, just dust.

The assistant helps Aldemar sit just behind the driver as the bus swerves avoiding potholes. Aldemar's knuckles are white; his right hand holds the metal frame of the driver's seat, and with the other he holds the black shoes with laces on his lap. His gaze fixed on them. He has never travelled on his own, and he has never owned a pair of shoes.

When he finds courage to observe around, he sees: a miniature Colombian flag, a lime green alarm clock that hangs by a piece of string; it spins next to a photograph of the Virgin Del Carmen who seems sad with the child in her arms, so he ties and unties the laces.

In the morning, Alicia had helped him wash his hair with soap, and dress in his Sunday best – a pair of brown shorts and a red checked shirt. And when he went into the unpainted room that served as a bedroom and sitting room, a toddler was playing with a broken little red truck, and in the corner the baby was howling in a hammock. His little black feet kicked out in rhythm with the cries. Umberto was sitting on a plastic chair, his jaw on his chest moving sideways, looking at his hands, picking dirt from his nails.

"I am not your papa, I am your uncle," Umberto said out of the blue.

"When your mother died I took you in. You were three. Your mother was a cook on a cattle ranch."

Aldemar heard the words coming out of his father's mouth hissing, hard. They echo too. The same way as when playing he covered his head with a large pan and shouted.

"Can I go to play football?" he asked.

"No this time, you need to grow up, you're seven. You can live with my sister, Oliva, in Cartagena."

Aldemar stayed quiet; he felt too old to cry.

On the bus, he feels a knot in his throat and his eyes sting. Umberto can't take him to the new job. It was the perfect job, but the new boss wanted a maximum of two children. His tone of voice was strange.

"Hola! Hola!" He lifts his eyes and meets the assistant's eyes.

"We're stopping for half an hour," he says.

Aldemar thinks about his shoes, but his bladder is full. He has to go, so he places his shoes under his seat. He gets off and goes in search of a toilet but as soon as he does he remembers Umberto's warning: "Be careful, there are kidnappers about." So he stays close to the bus, and is happy to walk behind a big nearby mango tree where he pees. And without losing time he climbs back onto the bus and checks under his seat, nothing. His shoes aren't there. He looks around thinking he has made a mistake but catches the assistant watching him. A sharp heat rushes to his face that forces him sit down. He feels transfixed and frightened by the smile on the assistant's face that becomes more of a smirk as he meets his eyes.

"What can I do?" he asks himself. Aldemar spends the remainder of the journey with his eyes rigidly on his lap as if the shoes were there. He wants Umberto and Alicia. She had made him stand on newspaper a few weeks back to trace his feet, tickling his feet and laughing at his big, bare, and hungry belly. In desperation, he wants to pray but doesn't know how. The swinging photograph of the Virgin reminds him of his mother, but memories of her are confined to small fragments and dreams, "Look at this apricot, it's big and yellow. Here, eat it quickly!" In another, she found him in the ashes with the cat next to the cooker, she laughed, full throated.

"Cartagena Terminal!" The assistant shouts. Aldemar's body jolts when the driver tries to avoid huge potholes.

"Bloody roads! Bloody politicians!" the driver says. Aldemar feels sick. His eyes concentrate on the brown of his shorts. He ignores the whirrs, the beeps, and the toots and when he dares to look outside, he sees: more buses, cars, bikes, and people. In a pothole, a seagull squashed so many times that there is only the shape of it with feathers, as if they were stuck with glue. He can't breathe; hot waves of dizziness hit him.

At the terminal, passengers descend to raucous noise and mayhem. Aldemar doesn't move from his seat. The assistant gets near him, "We're here," he says. Aldemar doesn't answer. "Okay?" the assistant asks.

"Where are they?" Aldemar asks without looking up. The assistant lowers his head and scratches it as if he does not understand.

"Where're my shoes?" Aldemar asks, but this time he looks in the assistant's eyes, "Where are they?"

He stands.

"They're here," the assistant says reaching into the compartment above the driver's seat.

CONTRIBUTORS

Olga Alexandru

Olga Alexandru is a Romanian-Canadian writer currently living in Bristol, UK. She makes zines and writes poetry as a form of self care and exploration. Her dream is to build and live in a tiny house on a tropical island. She was sick of being told that no one publishes confessional poetry, so she's proving them wrong.

Karolina Kew

Karolina Kew is a playwright and author. Her short plays Rosebush Park and Starlight were performed at fringe festivals in Plymouth and Swindon and her story Disturbance was published in a Bristol Festival of Literature competition.

Paul David Holland

Paul David Holland is a writer and artist based in Corsham, who has always been fascinated by languages and words. Although by day he is Head of Classics at Westonbirt School, he is currently working on a collection of fantasy stories, a psychological thriller and a series of essays based on his travel experiences.

www.pauldavidholland.co.uk
Twitter: @stcretiens/@TruthAtlantis

Tanya Almeida

To most of the world Tanya Almeida might appear as a geek, but she has a secret life as a writer. It started when visually vivid imagination erupted onto paper in the form of flash fiction. She is currently working on her first novel about one woman's desire for love, family and identity. She attends a weekly writing group for critique, encouragement and the joy of hearing stories being created.

talesfromtanya.wordpress.com

Gerard Twomey

Gerard Twomey is an archaeologist and drummer. He is a Screenwriting graduate of the Northern Film School, and a documentary film maker specialising in archaeology. He writes Fantasy and Science Fiction stories and screenplays. He is currently writing a future fantasy novel

David Turnbull

David Turnbull is Scottish by birth but has lived in London most of his adult life. He is a member of the Clockhouse London group of genre writers. He writes mainly short fiction and has had numerous short stories published in magazines and anthologies.

www.tumsh.co.uk

Benjamin F Jones

Benjamin F Jones is a writer working in South Wales. He loves pizza, photography and moist clay. When it rains he catches drops in his open mouth. He creates poetry, short fiction and absurdist snapshots. He is currently hiding in a warehouse, exploring photography and planning an expedition to the bottom of the garden with his woodlouse.

https://graphitebunny.wordpress.com/

Gavin Ritchie

Gavin Ritchie, born and raised a Fifer, is an author of short-form prose and poetry, but that's just a cover for his underground work as a soothsayer and novelist. His first book, a four-part beast set in 2055, is brewing somewhere in Bristol, where he also teaches English.

sinsinminkin.wordpress.com
Twitter: @sinsinminkin

Emily Tremmis

Emily Tremmis lives by the sea with her cat, where she writes magic realism short stories, and is working on a novel about a princess and a dragon-girl.

https://www.tumblr.com/blog/emilycorentine

Rosalie Alston

Rosalie Alston has personal experience of adoption and of finding brothers and sisters as an adult. As a social worker, she has supported adult Australian child migrants searching for their families of origin. From the 1940s to 1970s, many of these children had been placed in British orphanages by their mothers, who believed that their children were being placed for adoption locally.

Rosalie has heard adults express their profound sense of loss and powerlessness when as children they were sent to an unknown, far away country without their families' knowledge, often led to believe that they were orphans. Rosalie has a passion for writing and has had several poems published, including about adoption. As a social worker, she is currently involved in finding adoptive families for siblings so that brothers and sisters can stay together.

She facilitates Writing for Well-Being for adoptive families and believes in the power of writing to connect with people, bringing healing, affirmation and inspiration.

DM Tomkins

DM Tomkins is passionate about the environment and writes novels and short stories dealing with climate change and family relationships.

In January 2017 she set up Bristol Climate Writers, which offers support and critique for writers of all genres and all types of writing, including fiction, journalism, nature writing and poetry.

She is also a member of ClimateCultures, a network of artists and scientists, and has been involved in Bristol Festival of Literature.

Twitter: @tomkins deborah
Facebook: BristolClimateWriters

Lisa Lopresti

Lisa Lopresti is a West Country poet who lives in the ship shape and Bristol fashion city and manages a homeless hostel for families. In her spare time, (when she is not scribbling down poetry, some submitted and published or to languish in her kitchen drawers, though a few shared with iPhone photos on tumblr) is foraging for ingredients to turn into, hopefully, beautiful home-made wine or her favourite Elder-flower Champagne. The strength of human spirit and regular trips to the Devon and Cornish coasts has always inspired her.

Tumblr - shipshapewithsliders

Tara Lynn Masih

Tara Lynn Masih has won multiple book awards in her role as editor of The Rose Metal Press Field Guide to Writing Flash Fiction and The Chalk Circle: Intercultural Prizewinning Essays. She is also author of Where the Dog Star Never Glows: Stories and Founding Series Editor for The Best Small Fictions annual anthology. Awards for her work include The Ledge Magazine's Fiction Award, the Lou P. Bunce Creative Writing Award, a Neville Award citation, and Pushcart Prize, Best New American Voices, and Best of the Web nominations. "Scent of *Qahwa*" was exhibited in the 2016 Compassion, Creativity, and Courage Exhibit to Benefit Amirah.

http://taramasih.com/
https://www.goodreads.com/author/show/2889627.Tara_Lynn_Masih
https://www.amazon.com/Tara-L-Masih/e/B00383VGOU
https://www.linkedin.com/in/tara-lynn-masih-1a403825/
https://www.facebook.com/tara.masih.1

P.J. Reed

P.J. Reed is a writer and poet from England. She holds a BAEd from Canterbury Christ Church University, an MA from Bradford University and has dabbled in Psychology at the OU. She is an outrageously eclectic writer.
Her work has appeared in a wide variety of online and print magazines, collections, anthologies and podcasts. In 2015 she was shortlisted for the National Poetry Anthology award. Her haiku collections include - Haiku Nation, Frozen Haiku, Flicker and Haiku Yellow.
'The Dark Tales of Witherleigh' her sinister thriller based on a remote Devon village is available to download from Radish Publications.
'Defiance' the first instalment of The Torcian Chronicles, her high fantasy magical adventure series will be published Spring 2018.

http://fantasyworlds.jigsy.com
Twitter: @PJReed_author
Facebook: https://www.facebook.com/p.j.reedauthor/

Merlin Goldman

Merlin Goldman is a Londoner, trained as a biochemical engineer, writing high concept stories. This is usually in the form of prose, plays and film/tv scripts. His preferred genres are crime thrillers (Sea Glass, The Proving), drama (Tick-Tock, Tank, Mug Punt, Moonies, Travel Sick) and science fiction (Tokyo Violet, Orbital).

www.magnetical.com
Twitter: @mhgoldman
Facebook: https://www.facebook.com/magneticalwriting/

Mike Evis

Mike Evis lives just outside Oxford. He is a former software engineer with a long standing interest in writing – as well as a chronic inability to pass any bookshop without entering and buying at least one book. A wide ranging reader, his interests include modern literature, science fiction, fantasy, and thrillers. He escapes from books by going walking in the Oxfordshire countryside. He also likes obscure indie music no one has ever heard of. His stories have appeared in a number of anthologies.

Luke Palmer

Luke Palmer is based in Wiltshire. He has been a Secondary English Teacher for 10 years and is a poetry reviewer for the Journal of the National Association of Writers in Education. His poems have been published in Orbis, the Agenda Broadsheets and he was an Agenda New Generation Poet in 2016. Luke's work is concerned with trauma, the dislocation of memory, and the preservation of fractal experience.

Twitter: @lcpalmerpoet

Alice Little

Inspired by literary fiction of the early twentieth century, Alice enjoys writing of all kinds: it helps that she has beautiful handwriting and lots of nice stationery. She has had seven short stories published and is currently working on a piece of longer fiction.

alicelittle.co.uk/fiction
Twitter: @littleamiss

Helen Sheppard

Helen is fascinated by birth and right to be heard.
Inspired by her work as a midwife.
Co-runs and Poet in Residence at Satellite of Love Spoken word events.
Published in: Anthology Hippocrates Prize (2017), No Tribal Dance (2017),
Online: I Am Not A Silent Poet and Blue of Noon.
Poem 'Opening' Commended in Hippocrates Prize for Poetry and Medicine 2017
Recently performed her poems at The Nuyorican Poets Cafe NYC.

https://www.writeoutloud.net/profiles/helensheppard
Twitter: @HelenSheppard7

Lindsay Oliver

Lindsay Oliver began writing and performing at open mic nights in 2013 after she retired due to ill-health and disability. She writes poetry, short stories and longer fiction. Her poetry has been published in print and online journals and blogs including Lallans: The Journal of the Scots Language Society, Thank You for Swallowing, I am not a silent poet, Poetry24 and Forage.

http://lindsayoliver.scot/
https://twitter.com/imLindsayOliver

Aziz Dixon

Aziz Dixon draws on local Pennine and Welsh landscapes and life experiences. He explores the sacred in life through themes of love, music, landscape and wildlife. He has been published in 'Pennine Ink' and internationally online.
Aziz has poems forthcoming in Best of Bolton (November), The Curlew and in Perspectives. Aziz recently read at the RS Thomas Festival, Eglwysfach in September, and at the Burnley Literary Festival in October.

https://www.amazon.co.uk/Poet-Emerging-Aziz-Dixon/dp/1533691177/

Marc Nash

Marc Nash has published five collections of Flash Fiction and his fifth novel will be published by Dead Ink Books early 2018. He has also been published by Akashic Books, Culture Matters, The Good Men project, London Literary Project Spontaneity, Hypnopomp and the Rough Guide To Rock. He also works with video makers to turn some of his flash fiction into digital storytelling in the form of kinetic typography animated stories. An excellent live performer he won the 2014 Brighton Digital festival Flash Slam. He lives and works in London for a Free Expression NGO.

http://sulcicollective.blogspot.co.uk
Twitter: @21stCscribe

Mary Prior

Mary Prior started writing about ten years ago and got hooked. Since then she has had both poetry and short stories published. She is currently editing a dystopian novel for 8-12 year olds and is working on an historical novel set in Victorian England. Her enthusiasms are family, lurchers, gardening and reading and listening to a wide variety of writing in all genres.

marypriorwriter.com

Diana Brighouse

Diana Brighouse came late to writing after a successful career as a doctor. She has always read widely, particularly enjoying contemporary literary fiction. She is currently completing an MA in Creative Writing at the University of Chichester. Her diverse interests include psychoanalysis and premier league football.

www.dianabrighouse.com
Twitter: @dianabrighouse

Angie Belcher

Angie is a stand- up comedian, script writer and poet .Her Edinburgh show "Mythical Creature" won Best Spoken Word Show and she was a finalist in UK Best Comedy newcomer 2015. She wrote "What Has Shakespeare Ever Done for us?" a piece of touring public theatre and "My Funny Valentine" was featured on Radio 4. Angie was commissioned to write poetry for the Winter Olympics and her play Waiting For Pedro recently premiered in Bristol. Angie is currently touring her character poet "Odious Vex" and she is writer in residence for Severn Vale School in Gloucester and the WordUp programme.

www.angiebelcher.wordpress.com
Twitter: @angiebelcher
https://www.facebook.com/AngieBelcherComedian/

CB Baker

CB Baker is a writer who loves to be outdoors, drink lots of coffee, and indulge herself in the perfectly impossible word of fiction. She is in the process of creating her first book baby- 'Vanish'.

M M Lewis

M M Lewis is widely published in the independent press, including the British Fantasy Society Journal, Theaker's Quarterly and Wordland. He is currently working on a novel of urban magic. He lives by the sea in the South West of England. He is a member of the Clockhouse London Writers.

syntheticscribe.wordpress.com

Harry Greatorex

Harry Greatorex is a writer and researcher living in Bristol. He is winner of the 2012 Best and Brightest prize for short fiction. His debut novel How to Trump Brexit will be on sale in 2018.

Twitter: @htgreatorex

Tess Clare Lily

Tess is a spirited writer who uses her energy and imagination as a creative outlet in her spare time. A love of storytelling has led Tess to begin working on her first novel. Her fascination with the resilience of the human spirit and the complexities of the human mind spill into her writing and she is inspired by human psychology and what makes people real.

Twitter: @tessc_a

Maggie Elliott

Maggie Elliott, originally from Airdrie, is a retired secretary who lives in Oxfordshire. She knits for charity and writes purely for pleasure. She won third prize for her poem 'Picture Me Calm' in the Swanwick Writers poetry competition in June 2017.
She loves animals, particularly cats, listening to holistic music (David Sun, Deuter etc) and watching comedies on television.

Facebook – Maggie Elliott and AirdrieLady Knits

Linda M. Crate

Linda M. Crate is an author, writer, and poet whose works have been published in numerous anthologies and magazines both online and in print. When she isn't writing she enjoys reading, spending time with family and friends, being out in nature, photography, anime, museums, learning about history and art, swimming, and finding beauty in unlikely places.

Twitter @thysilverdoe
https://www.instagram.com/authorlindamcrate/
https://www.facebook.com/Linda-M-Crate-129813357119547/
https://www.goodreads.com/author/show/
8122996.Linda_M_Crate

Clare Evans

Clare Evans has had a varied career covering IT, Marketing, Management and full time motherhood and has always squeezed writing into the spaces that remain.

In Autumn 2016 she took the plunge and studied for a full time MA in Creative Writing at Bath Spa University.

She is currently writing a novel, Tangled Roots, that explores the dangers of secrets in family relationships and uses a garden as a character and a medium for communication.

Twitter: @Ctsixpence

Richard Devereux

Richard Devereux is a member of Lansdown Poets and Bristol Stanza. His collection Bill tells the story of his grandfather, a soldier of World War One who fought on the Balkan front in northern Greece. Richard taught English in Athens and his knowledge of Greece inspires and informs much of his writing. His poems have appeared in several anthologies and on-line magazines.

Alexander MJ Smith

Alexander MJ Smith has always been a writer, but it's taken him until his mid-twenties to own up to it. Right now he's either writing a script for his portfolio (with which he hopes to enter the film and television industry) or exploring the South West coast and deciding what to write next. In either case, there's coffee involved and he's probably going to get distracted by the surf forecast.

Shell Marriott

Michelle lives in muddy Weston-super-Mare with her two teenagers and a small cat called Mugs. Her eclectic career has included jobs as a cleaner, dispensing chemist, and farm hand, but she is now studying for an MA in Literature, Landscape and the Environment at Bath Spa University. She enjoys searching for ruins in the Somerset Levels, collecting stamps, and has a strange phobia of Maltesers. Her love of poetry was inspired by her Mother, who taught her how to treasure words, and to treat them like little pieces of art.

Tim Burroughs

Tim is a poet who lives, writes and performs in Bristol.

He has been published in numerous anthologies.
His last collection was "Lament For Gaia - A Poet's Journey In Eco Consciousness" - a stark warning about global warning.
He has recorded his poems on a Cd "Soundings" and set to his music on another "Soundscapes".

He hosts SPEL, an alt poetry open mic, and co-hosts The Berkeley Square Poetry Revue.
He has a website on I Page and on Facebook("Tim Burroughs Poetry" and "Tim Burroughs Poet").

He has performed at many poetry events including the Bristol Folk Fest and Edinburgh Fringe. His poems have been made into films by Diana Taylor.

Ruby Vallis

Ruby Vallis's love for reading and writing is rooted in her childhood. It was an inauspicious start. She was born in Cajamarca, Colombia, at a time when the education of girls was not always considered a priority. When she was five years old her father, an illiterate farmer, told her that she would not be going to school – she remembers feeling sad about this, but at the time did not understand why. As she was to be denied an education, she shadowed her two older brothers, and learned to read and write even before they did. From that point on, reading and writing became a passion and a source of empowerment. She went on to read Economics at Westminster University, but it was not until recent years she was able to pursue one part of her dream. In 2007 she began a degree in English Literature at Bath Spa University, and in 2017 finished a Masters in Creative Writing.

Tony D'Arpino

Tony D'Arpino is an American poet living in England (Leave to Remain visa). His most recent book of poetry is Floating Harbour (Redcliffe Press). Other work has appeared in Agenda, Barrow Street, The Clearing, E-Ratio, The North, and the Glasgow Review of Books.

Hannah M Rudd

Hannah loves words, especially if they've been plucked out from languages' jumble and trained to engage, inspire and delight. Having studied writing at Plymouth University and practised it as a copywriter in Lima and Bristol, Hannah now works as a bid writer and uses words to generate charitable income. Apart from that, Hannah likes to go on adventures and read by torchlight.

https://ringladytraining.wordpress.com

Saili Katebe

Saili Katebe is a Zambian writer, poet and spoken word artist. Born in Zambia, he moved to the UK in his early teens. His work is influenced by his experiences of both cultures, exploring language in both the spoken and written form, he explores the space in which the two cultures meet.

EDITOR'S NOTE

Thank you for reading *Voices along the Road*. We hope you enjoyed it.

If you're a sci-fi fan and would like to contribute to the charity *and* get another great read into the bargain, you might be interested in *Another Place,* a collection of science fiction short stories. Like *Voices along the Road,* all profits are donated to the Alf Dubs Children's Fund.

If you'd like to find out more about the great work that the Alf Dubs Children's Fund does, visit:
http://safepassage.org.uk/what-we-do/alf-dubs-fund/

27609221R00070

Printed in Great Britain
by Amazon